SPEEDY BOSH!

SIGNED BY THE AUTHORS

PUBLISHED BY HQ
SEPTEMBER 2020

Welcome to this super-exclusive
edition of SPEEDY BOSH!,
with six fantastic bonus
recipes created just for you.

SPEEDY
BOSH!

Purple Berry Smoothie Bowl

Fridge-Raid Veggie Soup

Beetroot Pesto Risotto

Stifado and Mash

Spinach and Feta Bourekas

Almond and Berry Dipping Cookies

Purple Berry Smoothie Bowl

A fruit-packed smoothie is always a great way to start the day, but served in a bowl and beautifully adorned with more fresh fruit, nuts and seeds, and it immediately becomes a celebratory, weekend-worthy breakfast that's wonderfully healthy and well worth taking the time over. Once you have all your ingredients to hand, this really is just a case of whizzing the smoothie up in a blender, pouring it into bowls and garnishing it with your favourite toppings. So simple and so delicious.

Makes 2

2 frozen bananas
300g frozen mixed berries
25g vanilla protein powder (optional)
6 tbsp unsweetened plant-based milk
2 tbsp maple syrup

To serve (mix & match)
2 tbsp pumpkin seeds
2 tbsp cacao nibs or
    dark chocolate chips
4 heaped tbsp granola
handful of mixed nuts
2 handfuls fresh mixed berries

Take the bananas out of the freezer to thaw slightly • Nutribullet or other power blender

Make the smoothie • Peel the frozen bananas • Add all the smoothie ingredients to the blender • Blend for 1 minute, then scrape down the sides of the blender to ensure all of the ingredients are well incorporated • Blend again until smooth

To serve • Divide the smoothie between 2 bowls • Top with the pumpkin seeds, cacao nibs or chocolate chips, granola, mixed nuts and fresh berries

Fridge-Raid Veggie Soup

Nourishing, warming and delicious, this substantial soup makes a great rustle-up meal for those times when you have a fridge full of vibrant veg and want to get something tasty and healthy on the table with minimal fuss. Feel free to mix up the vegetables and herbs to work with the seasons and use up whatever you have in the fridge. Serve with a generous hunk of sourdough to soak up the delicious broth and you've got yourself a sustaining, flavour-packed meal in no time.

Serves 2

1 red onion
2 tbsp olive oil
handful of fresh rosemary, thyme
    and/or sage leaves (ideally all 3)
1 bay leaf
1 tsp fennel seeds
2 garlic cloves
1 large or 2 medium ripe Italian
    tomatoes or 2 handfuls
    cherry tomatoes
generous pinch of salt
1 x small (125ml) glass red
    or white wine
1 small carrot
1 small courgette
handful of kale or cavolo nero
½ x 400g tin beans (any type)
500ml hot vegetable stock

To serve
handful of fresh basil leaves
plant-based parmesan
drizzle of olive oil
black pepper
crusty sourdough

Large saucepan over a medium heat

Make the soup • Peel and finely slice the onion • Heat the olive oil in the hot saucepan • Add the onion to the pan with the herbs, bay leaf and fennel seeds and stir for about 5 minutes • Peel and finely slice the garlic cloves and add them to the pan • Roughly chop the tomatoes and add to the pan with the salt • Stir to release the tomato juices • Increase the heat and add the glass of wine • Bring to a simmer and let the wine bubble and reduce for 3–4 minutes • Peel the carrot, and then shave strips directly into the pan • Reduce the heat to low and shave the courgette into the pan in ribbons • Trim and finely slice the kale or cavolo nero and add it to the pan, pressing it down into the juices • Drain the beans and add them with the hot stock • Reduce the heat to its lowest setting and simmer for just a few minutes

To serve • Spoon a generous portion of soup into each bowl • Tear over the basil leaves, shave over some parmesan, sprinkle with plenty of pepper and drizzle with olive oil • Cut thick wedges of bread – we like throwing chunks into the soup to soak it up!

Beetroot Pesto Risotto

'Eating the rainbow' is a great mantra if you want to eat healthily because it's really important to get loads of colourful veggies into your diet. This dish is incredibly colourful. The green asparagus and red beetroot not only look good together, but they taste great together, too. If you're into beetroot, this speedy risotto will be right up your street.

Serves 2

200g risotto rice
600ml vegetable stock
2 tbsp olive oil
½ onion
2 garlic cloves
175ml white wine
1 x 250g pack cooked beetroot
200g asparagus
salt

For the beetroot pesto

40g pumpkin seeds
1 lemon
1 tbsp nutritional yeast
2 tbsp olive oil
salt and black pepper

To serve

30g dairy-free crème fraîche
small bunch of fresh dill

Preheat grill to high • **Line a baking tray** • **Large saucepan on a medium-high heat** • **Frying pan on a medium-high heat** • **Microplane or fine grater** • **Food processor**

Give the risotto a head start • Tip the rice and 300ml of the stock into the hot saucepan • Cover and cook for 5 minutes, stirring occasionally to stop it sticking to the pan

Finish the risotto • Heat 1 tablespoon of the olive oil in the frying pan • Peel and finely chop the onion and add it to the pan with a big pinch of salt • Fry for 2 minutes • Peel the garlic cloves and grate them directly into the pan • Pour in the wine and bring to the boil • Tip the contents of the frying pan into the risotto pan • Pour in the remaining stock • Give everything a good stir • Lower the heat to medium, cover and cook for 8–10 minutes

Grill the beets and asparagus • Drain and roughly chop half the beetroot • Tip onto the baking tray • Trim any woody ends from the asparagus and add it to the tray • Drizzle with the remaining 1 tablespoon of olive oil and season with salt • Place under the hot grill for 5 minutes, turning occasionally until browned all over

Meanwhile, make the beetroot pesto • Put the frying pan back on a high heat • Scatter over the pumpkin seeds and toast until they start to pop • Set aside a small handful and tip the rest into the food processor • Add the remaining beets to the processor • Halve the lemon and squeeze in the juice • Add the nutritional yeast and olive oil • Blitz to a paste • Season to taste with salt and pepper and stir through the risotto, mixing everything together well.

Serve • Spoon the risotto into bowls • Top with the roasted asparagus and beets, and a dollop of dairy-free crème fraîche • Scatter over the dill fronds and reserved seeds

Stifado & Mash

Perhaps the most hearty, warming dish in this book, this *stifado* (Greek for stew) is rich, comforting and packed with earthy umami flavours. Mushrooms take pride of place as the perfect hero ingredient – delicious and packed with goodness. In true BOSH! style, we've added a delicious and quick creamy mash to soak up all the delicious stew. This is a firm favourite in our kitchen, so cook it up and take yourself on a culinary trip to the taverna.

Serves 2

1 onion
2 tbsp olive oil
2 bay leaves
2 garlic cloves
handful of fresh rosemary sprigs
2 cloves
handful of sultanas
2 tsp ground allspice
1 tsp ground cinnamon
1 tbsp soy sauce
250g chestnut mushrooms
1 tbsp tomato purée
200g passata
salt and black pepper

For the spring onion mash
1 large baking potato
dash of oat milk
dash of olive oil
2 spring onions
salt and black pepper

For the cucumber salad
½ cucumber
pinch of salt
dash of white wine vinegar
dash of sesame oil
sprinkle of sesame seeds
    (toasted, if liked)
handful of fresh mint
    or 1 tsp dried mint

Medium saucepan • Kettle boiled • Large, deep frying pan on a medium heat • Pestle and mortar • Masher • Grater

Start with the spring onion mash • Peel and roughly chop the potato • Add to the saucepan, cover with boiling water and add some salt • Set over a high heat, bring to the boil and simmer for 10–15 minutes until soft

Make the stifado • Peel and finely slice the onion • Add half the olive oil to the hot frying pan • Add the onion and bay leaves to the hot oil • Peel the garlic cloves and put them in the mortar with the rosemary sprigs and cloves • Bash together, then add the sultanas, allspice, cinnamon, soy sauce and remaining tablespoon of olive oil • Bash everything together until you have a dark paste, then add this to the onions and stir • Cut the mushrooms into quarters and add them to the pan • Stir in the tomato purée and let everything merge together for a few minutes

Return to the mash • Drain the potato, reserving 300ml of the starchy water • Tip the potato back into the pan and add the oat milk, salt, pepper and olive oil • Mash until smooth • Slice or snip the spring onions over the top

Return to the stifado • Add the reserved potato water and the passata to the pan of onions and mushrooms • Stir and taste for seasoning • Lower the heat, if necessary, and leave to simmer while you make the salad

For the cucumber salad • Halve the cucumber lengthways and scoop out and discard the watery seeds • Roughly grate into a bowl • Add the salt, white wine vinegar, sesame oil and sesame seeds and mix together • Finely slice the mint and scatter it over the top or sprinkle with dried mint

To serve • Spoon the mash into a wide bowl • Ladle the stifado next to it and top with a spoonful of cucumber salad

Spinach & Feta Bourekas

These moreish morsels of tangy dairy-free feta, earthy spinach and fragrant herbs all wrapped in deliciously crunchy filo pastry make great canapés or party snacks, but would also make a wonderful addition to a mezze platter (see page 142) or could be served with either of the couscous salads in this book. However you choose to serve them, one thing's for sure, they won't last long!

Makes 12

6 sheets filo pastry
2 tbsp olive oil

For the filling
300g frozen spinach
50g pitted olives
1 lemon
2 garlic cloves
200g dairy-free feta
2 tsp nutritional yeast
a generous grating of nutmeg
30g almonds
10g fresh mint
10g fresh parsley
generous pinch each salt and
    black pepper

For the sesame wash
½ tsp tahini
1 tbsp unsweetened plant-based milk
1 tbsp olive oil
1 tbsp sesame seeds

Thaw the pastry, if necessary • Preheat oven to 200°C • Colander • Large food processor • Line a baking tray with baking paper • Whisk • Pastry brush

Make the filling • Place the frozen spinach in a colander and run under warm water until thawed • Using your hands, squeeze as much water as possible from the spinach, leaving you with a drained weight of about 100g • Tip the spinach into the food processor • Lay the olives on a couple of sheets of kitchen paper and roll them to remove excess moisture, then add to the food processor • Zest the lemon and cut in half • Peel the garlic • Add the lemon zest and a squeeze of the juice to a food processor, then add all the other filling ingredients • Blitz until smooth

Make the bourekas • Place 1 sheet of filo pastry on a board with the long side toward you • Brush all over with olive oil, then lay another sheet of pastry on top • Cut the pastry sheets in half down the middle, then cut each piece in half again, leaving you with 4 long, thin rectangles • Spoon 1 tablespoon of the filling mixture onto each rectangle at the end closest to you, leaving at small gap at the edges of the pastry • Roll up to form cigar shapes • Place on the lined baking tray – it doesn't matter if they are touching • Repeat twice more until all the pastry and filling is used up

Make the sesame wash • Whisk all the ingredients together in a bowl

To finish • Brush all of the sesame wash mixture over the cigars • Bake in the oven for 15–18 minutes, until golden and crisp • Remove from the oven and serve

Almond & Berry Dipping Cookies

Cookies. Nuts. Chocolate. Need we say more? For an adult twist on a childhood classic, these delicious, speedy treats are spiked with almonds, cherries and berries and made even more special with the addition of an indulgent chocolate dipping sauce. If you don't want to bake the whole batch in one go, portion the dough into cookies and freeze any you don't want to cook that day for later. Then simply defrost and bake them whenever your inner Cookie Monster comes calling.

Makes 14

100g caster sugar
125g light muscovado or brown sugar
150g plant-based butter
1 tsp vanilla extract
1½ tsp cider vinegar
250g plain flour
good pinch of sea salt
1 tsp baking powder
½ tsp bicarbonate of soda
35g flaked almonds
70g dried berries

To serve
100g dairy-free chocolate

Preheat oven to 170°C • Line 2 baking sheets with baking paper • Electric hand-held beaters • Small microwaveable bowl • Microwave

Make the dough • Pour the sugars into a large mixing bowl and crumble out any lumps • Add the plant-based butter and beat until creamy with the electric beaters (don't over-mix, it doesn't need to be too aerated) • Beat in the vanilla, cider vinegar and 1 tablespoon of the flour • Add the rest of the flour, the salt, baking powder and bicarbonate of soda to a second bowl and mix to combine • Add the dry mixture to the creamy mixture and fold together gently, then briefly beat with the electric beaters until the mixture is evenly combined • Roughly chop the almonds and fold them in along with the dried berries

Bake the cookies • Scoop 14 evenly sized balls of dough onto the lined baking sheets, spacing them well apart • Bake for 12–15 minutes, until just slightly squidgy in the middles (the baking sheet on the bottom shelf may need the longer cooking time) • Remove from the oven and let cool on the baking sheets for 5–10 minutes

To serve • Melt the chocolate in the microwave in 30 second bursts • Serve alongside the cookies for dipping

SPEEDY
BOSH

SPEEDY
BOSH!

QUICK • EASY • ALL PLANTS

NUMBER 1 BESTSELLING AUTHORS
HENRY FIRTH & IAN THEASBY

HQ
An imprint of HarperCollins*Publishers* Ltd
1 London Bridge
London SE1 9GF

10 9 8 7 6 5 4 3 2 1

First published in Great Britain by HQ
An imprint of HarperCollins*Publishers* Ltd 2020

Text Copyright © Henry Firth and Ian Theasby 2020

Design and Photography Copyright © HQ, an imprint
of HarperCollins*Publishers* Ltd 2020

Henry Firth and Ian Theasby assert the moral right to be identified as
the authors of this work. A catalogue record for this book is available
from the British Library.

ISBN 978-0-00-833293-8

For more information visit: www.harpercollins.co.uk/green

Photography (food): Lizzie Mayson
Photography (portrait): Nicky Johnston
Food Styling: Elena Silcock
Prop Styling: Sarah Birks
Design and Art Direction: Studio Polka
Editorial Director: Rachel Kenny
Project Editor: Daniel Hurst
Head of Design: Kate Oakley

Cover Design: HQ 2020

Printed and bound in Italy by Rotolito S.p.A.

Contents

Welcome

Woah, has the world changed since we published our first book! More people than ever before are deciding to fill their plates with delicious veggies. Shops are stocking a better variety of awesome vegan staples – it's not all veggie sausages now. And when it comes to plant-based dishes, restaurants have a lot more than just mushroom risotto on the menu. (Mind you, as we write this, the restaurants are closed for a pandemic lockdown, so we've all been making our own mushroom risotto!)

Of course, we can't ignore that a big part of why we're seeing this global movement towards plant-based eating is because the planet is suffering, and that's scary. But we have the privilege of living at a point in human history when we can really do something about climate change. How beautiful is that? We're not scientists or climate experts, but we do know studies show that the single biggest way we can reduce our impact on the Earth is by eating less meat and dairy. And we are glad to have played a small part in getting people excited about changing their eating habits, even if it's just for a couple of meals a week.

But we want to do more. A lot more. We want to make it even easier for you to eat tasty, satisfying, plant-based food, especially because there's a bit of a misconception that vegan food takes a long time to make. So, we thought we'd address that head-on.

We've come up with this mouthwatering collection of dishes you can get on the table in 30 minutes or less (with some of them you'll even have time left over to do the washing up!). They are perfect for weeknight dinners after a long day, speedy breakfasts to supercharge the family or for Sunday prep for the week of meals ahead.

In this book we have the classics that we promise you'll be turning to again and again: fragrant curries, indulgent puds and sweet treats, wonderful hearty stews, comfort food for when the cold nights start drawing in – because, YES, vegan food absolutely can be comforting, just have a taste of our mac & cheese or lasagne, our outrageously good rice and noodle dishes, bountiful sharing platters, one-pan wonders and grab-and-go food to make you feel energised.

You'll need no fancy kit and no out-there ingredients. You'll be able to get all the bits and pieces you need from your nearest large supermarket, and everything has been tried and tested to make sure that we are never, ever, compromising on flavour. Never let vegan food be called bland, because, honestly, this might just be our tastiest collection of recipes yet, as well as our quickest. And of course, as with all our books, every single recipe has an accompanying photo because, we get it, you need to see what you're aiming for, right?

So, come on, dive in. These recipes are our pride and joy and we can't wait to hear what you think of them. And remember… one plate at a time, we'll get there.

x Henry & Ian

About this book

Your time is the single most important thing you have in the world.

This book is a tribute to your time, the ultimate non-renewable resource. We're going to help you save it so you can spend more time doing the things you love. Or the things you don't love that need doing! That's always been our philosophy – with our videos, our recipes and our cookbooks.

If the time you have is a couple of lovely leisurely hours, then we believe that one of the best ways you can spend it is by making a lasagne with all the bells and whistles. But we know the drill, most days you're lucky if you can get 30 uninterrupted minutes to put together a meal out of the odds and ends in the fridge. And on those days, when it's dinnertime already, the kids are mardy and you're feeling a tad overwhelmed, that's where this book comes in. We've got you covered.

This time, we've gone all out and come up with over 100 cracking recipes with fewer steps, fewer ingredients, less prep and less cooking time, but still all the flavour. We're going to help you knock up something delicious in half an hour or under, and that includes prep time. Yes, you heard that right. It's not half an hour cooking time, with an hour of chopping veg, making marinades and crushing garlic before you even get started. It's not half an hour if you're a Michelin-starred chef who can chop an onion in 10 seconds flat. No. Instead, we guarantee that, provided you're not a complete beginner, you can hit the timer the second you've laid out all your ingredients and kit, and you'll have turned those ingredients into amazing food that you and your family will love by the time that timer gets to 30 minutes. (This doesn't include chilling time for some of the sweet treats, but we figured that was OK, since you can be eating your dinner while your pud is cooling!)

So, how have we done this? We want to let you in on a few little secrets – we call them hacks and shortcuts – lazy garlic from a jar, liberal use of the microwave to pre-cook veg... (see page 15 for more). Some people might call it cheating, but our take is that life's too short to spend every moment of free time peeling, chopping, measuring and washing up (unless that's what you want to do, of course!). Once a week, sure. Special occasions, definitely! But for everyday cooking? Nahhh. We've got lives to live, deadlines to smash, places to be.

Let's all cook more regularly, and more quickly, and save our precious time for the things that matter most.

How to cook fast

Cooking fast is easy; it's something we can all do. It's all about having your core ingredients in the fridge, cupboard or freezer, your essential kit clean and ready to go, your kitchen organised like a pro's, picking the right recipes and getting familiar with the shortcuts (we call them hacks) to make them even quicker.

Kit list

- A good, sharp knife
- A nice big chopping board
- Clean tea towels, including one to clean your chopping board with and to keep it stable on the worktop
- Whisk, spatula, tongs and wooden spoons, all in an easy-to-access place
- Non-stick, high-quality saucepans and frying pans of different shapes and sizes
- A few different sized baking trays and roasting tins
- A clever drying rack or stacking implement (for quick air-drying of kit – particularly important if you don't have a dishwasher)
- Several nice large bowls and platters for salads, prep and for family-style serving
- A few freezer bags or Tupperware containers, so you can prep ahead
- Cooking timer (or a friendly mobile phone assistant)
- A power blender and/or food processor – as good as you can afford

Shopping list

Oils & vinegars
oils: coconut • extra-virgin olive • light olive • rapeseed • vegetable • **vinegars:** apple cider • balsamic • white wine

Herbs & spices (fresh and dried)
sea salt • black pepper • **fresh herbs:** basil • coriander • flat-leaf parsley • mint • sage • **dried herbs:** fennel seeds • oregano • rosemary • mixed Italian herbs • **spices:** allspice • chilli flakes • cumin seeds • ground cinnamon • ground coriander • ground cumin • ground turmeric • nutmeg • paprika • smoked paprika • chilli powder • curry powder

Instant flavour hits
savoury/spicy: mango chutney • miso soup sachets or ramen broth • miso paste • mustard • nutritional yeast • quick curry pastes, such as plant-based Thai red and Thai green • soy sauce • sriracha sauce • stock cubes • Tabasco • tahini • tomato purée • **sweet:** Biscoff spread • coffee • dark chocolate • golden syrup • jam • maple syrup • peanut butter • pomegranate molasses • vanilla extract or vanilla bean paste

Plant-based dairy
coconut milk • oat cream • plant-based butter • plant-based milk • plant-based yoghurt • dairy-free cream cheese • dairy-free crème fraîche • plant-based parmesan • dairy-free sliced cheese

Dips
baba ganoush • guacamole • hummus (various flavours)

Vegetables (fresh or pre-prepped)
aubergines • beetroot • broccoli • carrots • fresh red and green chillies • cucumbers • fresh tomatoes • garlic • ginger • green beans • jarred artichokes and roasted peppers • leeks • mushrooms • onions, spring onions or shallots • parsnips • peas • peppers • potatoes • sweet potatoes • spinach • squash • sugar snap peas • sun-dried tomatoes • tinned tomatoes or passata

Fruits
apples • avocados • bananas • frozen mixed berries • frozen smoothie mix • lemons • limes • olives • oranges • pomegranates

Grains, beans & pulses
pasta & noodles: dried pasta (brown and white) • lasagne sheets • macaroni • spaghetti • noodles • **rice:** dried, brown and white • pre-cooked • risotto • **other grains:** couscous • porridge oats • quinoa • **beans & pulses:** baked beans • black beans • chickpeas • kidney beans • pre-cooked lentils

Nuts & Seeds
almonds • cashews • flaxseeds (linseeds) • hazelnuts • pecans • sesame seeds

Ready-made pastries & baking
flours: buckwheat • gram (chickpea) • plain • self-raising • **pastry:** filo • puff • shortcrust • **breads & dough:** breadcrumbs and panko breadcrumbs • burger and hot dog buns • flatbreads • pitta bread • pizza dough • **sugar & chocolate:** caster • icing • muscovado • cocoa powder

Plant-based proteins and alternatives
jackfruit • seitan steaks • soya mince • tempeh • tofu: firm and silken • veggie meatballs • vegan meaty burgers • veggie sausages

Naughty snacks
dairy-free biscuits • dairy-free ice cream • dairy-free squirty cream • Oreos • dairy-free croissants

Top tips for organisation

- Keep regular ingredients such as oils, salt, black pepper and dried chilli flakes handy
- Keep your blender within easy reach, with all the parts in one box (we keep ours out on the work surface for daily smoothies)
- Put labels on the front edges of your shelves so that you know where to find things. Don't be afraid to reorganise the kitchen if the space isn't working for you – go full Marie Kondo!
- Have an ingredients shopping list placed somewhere easily visible and keep it up-to-date with things you've run out of: maybe a whiteboard on your fridge or an app on your phone
- Wash your tea towels, oven gloves and cloths etc. once a week so they're always ready to be used
- Keep your spices and dried herbs organised and labelled, either in a drawer or spinnable rack, so the names of the spices are easy to read from above
- Do your washing up as you go, so you don't have to do loads at the end of the meal!

Speedy hacks

We have two types of hacks: cooking hacks and food hacks. Both crop up in recipes throughout this book, often more than once. They're an integral part of fast cooking the BOSH! way, and you can return to these shortcuts again and again whenever you cook, not just when you want to rustle up a *Speedy BOSH!* dish. They're so useful that we've pulled our favourite hacks together into a visual index so you can see them all at a glance whenever you need to remind yourself of the tricks of the trade, or just need some speedy inspiration.

Cooking hacks

First up, cooking hacks. These are all about your process and equipment.

Chop smaller...

...to cook veg quicker: tiny veg = speedy cooking!
Butternut Squash Carbonara with Crispy Sage (page 51)
Beetroot & Lentil Burger (page 102)
Quick Fried Biryani (page 124)

Use herb stems...

...to add depth of flavour, save time and reduce waste: Don't bother picking the leaves off fresh herbs with soft stems (like basil, parsley and coriander). Finely chop and add the stems instead.
Deep, Dark & Smoky Chilli (page 32)
Black Bean Mole with Salsa (page 78)

Speed up garlic & ginger...

...by grating it: use a microplane or fine grater to quickly grate peeled garlic bulbs and fresh ginger (you can even leave the ginger skin on). To save peeling garlic, just put the whole bulb in a garlic crusher. That way, the skin comes off super-easily.
Speedy Restaurant Ramen (page 97)
Aubergine & Lentil Meatball Pasta (page 30)
Frying Pan Samosa Pie (page 48)

Use a microwave...

...to pre-cook veg: the microwave can help you speed up roasties, jacket potatoes and root veg. Give them a blast for a few minutes in the microwave first before finishing them off in the oven or in a pan. Timings will depend on the veg and its size.
Cauliflower Schnitzel – 3 Ways (page 39)
Crispy Jacket Potatoes (page 68)

...to quickly melt: you can quickly melt butter, chocolate or peanut butter in just 30–60 seconds in a microwave.
Rice Krispie Donuts (page 211)
Spice Dust Chocolate Truffles (page 214)

Use a food processor...

...to finely chop veg: no need to spend ages finely chopping veg. Instead, simply throw them into a food processor and pulse. It's so quick and easy to chop this way!
Ivory Coast Squash & Peanut Stew (page 44)
Super Meaty Spag Bol (page 84)

...to make burger, falafel or meatball mixes: use your blender to quickly blitz together a burger mix.
Aubergine & Lentil Meatball Pasta (page 30)
Beetroot & Lentil Burger (page 102)
Rainbow Falafel (page 170)

Use a blender...

...to make a cashew cream: add soaked or boiled cashews to a high-powered blender to make a quick creamy sauce.
Ultimate Vegan Mac & Cheese (page 88)
Butternut Squash Carbonara with Crispy Sage (page 51)

...to make a speedy sorbet or ice cream: you can use a blender filled with frozen berries or bananas to quickly make instant sorbet or ice cream.
Red Velvet Sorbet (page 232)

...to make quick sauces, dips and dressings: add a handful of ingredients plus a liquid base to a small food processor or blender to quickly make a delicious sauce or dressing.
Black Olive Pesto Pasta (page 36)
Tofu Satay Kebabs with Fresh Herbs (page 168)

Pre-cook...

...to speed up risottos: give your risotto a head start by boiling your rice in stock for 5 minutes before beginning the slower risotto cooking process.
Lizzie's Lemon & Artichoke Risotto (page 73)

...to speed up lasagne: make a lasagne in minutes by breaking up the sheets and parboiling them, then draining before stirring through your ragu.
Henry's 30 Minute Lasagne (page 62)

Cook simultaneously...

...to bake quick pies: pre-bake your pastry in the oven at the same time as cooking your filling.
Frying Pan Samosa Pie (page 48)
Potato & Pickle Upside-Down Pie (page 76)

...to speed up an onion-based sauce: sauté the onion in a separate pan to the other ingredients.
Goulash & Dumplings (page 91)

...to make a rich stew or casserole: sauté your veg and simmer your sauce in separate pans so every component is cooked to perfection
Red Wine Cassoulet (page 80)

...to make your soup more substantial: make a gorgeous textured topping alongside your soup that you can add at the end to bulk it up
Crispy Mushroom Soup (page 74)

One-pot cooking...

...to make a speedy cookie in one pan: mix all the ingredients together and add to a frying pan to create a giant one-pan cookie ready in minutes. Go wild and experiment with your favourite ingredients.
Frying Pan Cookie (page 234)

...to cook your pasta and accompanying sauce: simply add pasta, tomato, leafy greens and any other non-root veg to a pan with the correct amount of water to make a simple one-pan pasta.
Simple One-Pot Spaghetti
(page 92)

...to boil and steam: while boiling veg, rice or pasta, place a colander on top to create a steamer pan to cook other veggies.
Thanksgiving Roast (page 52)
Green Shepherd's Pie (page 58)

Use the fridge and freezer...

...to quickly prep a dessert: a quick blast will chill or set a dessert in no time. Just be sure to remember to get it out!
Rice Krispie Donuts (page 211)
Banana Microwave Cake (page 207)
Spectaculoos Cupcakes (page 221)
D's Gooey Choconut Ganache (page 222)

...to cool your dips before serving: blending warms up dips, and no one wants warm dips!
Best Friends' Dippy Platter (page 174)

...to chill serving glasses before dishing up: chilled glasses look super-classy and they keep desserts cooler for longer
Red Velvet Sorbet (page 232)
Margarita Fizz (page 246)
De La Seoul Bloody Mary (page 251)

...to keep your cocktails ice-cold before serving: this also helps all the flavours infuse beautifully
Rosé Sangria (page 244)

Food hacks

Food hacks are all about making the components of dishes that traditionally take a long time (such as vegan béchamel sauce or the rich flavours that come from slow cooking) super speedy, and with delicious results.

To make it cheesy...

...make a melty cheese sauce: if you can't find a good melty vegan cheese, you can make your own by combining vegan cheddar cheese with plant-based milk and warming through.
Cheatball Marinara Sub (page 118)

...make a speedy béchamel: make a quick béchamel or white sauce with flour, oat cream and almond milk.
Happy Chick'n Parmo (page 61)
Greens Gratin (page 64)

...use nutritional yeast: to bring a cheesy flavour to creamy sauces.
Henry's 30 Minute Lasagne (page 62)
Ultimate Vegan Mac & Cheese (page 88)
Butternut Squash Carbonara with Crispy Sage (page 51)

Make quick sauce bases or broths...

...by making a quicker onion base: instead of sautéing onions, use spring onions or shallots.
Super Meaty Spag Bol (page 84)

...by using ready-made curry pastes: use shop-bought vegan pastes to cook up curries in minutes.
Speedy Laksa (page 126)
Thai Green Curry Bowls (page 121)
Naan Tikka Pizza (page 149)

...by thickening with cooking water: use the starchy water from pasta to thicken up sauces.
Butternut Squash Carbonara (page 51)
Black Olive Pesto Pasta (page 36)

...by creating a flavourful stock: make a stock to simulate the flavour of a long-simmered dish.
Deep, Dark & Smoky Chilli (page 32)

...to create a speedy noodle soup: Use shop-bought miso broth to create a speedy ramen.
Speedy Restaurant Ramen (page 97)

Use ready-made pastry & dough...

...to make speedy pizzas: use high-quality shop-bought vegan pizza dough.
Speedy Pizza – 3 Ways (page 159)

...to make Yorkshire puddings and savoury pies: unroll shop-bought vegan puff pastry and get it in the oven in minutes, then use it as a pie topper, base or even a replacement for Yorkshire pudding.
Cheat's Toad in the Hole with Curry Gravy (page 29)
Potato & Pickle Upside-Down Pie (page 76)

...to make healthier pie toppers: scrunch up filo pastry for a quick, healthy pie topping.
Frying Pan Samosa Pie (page 48)

...to make delicious desserts: use shop-bought vegan puff pastry to make a whole host of sweet treats.
Cronuts (page 208)
Coffee Caramel Tearer Sharer (page 218)
Frances' PBJ Pop Tarts (page 271)
Portuguese Custard Tarts (page 229)

Use instant, intense flavours...

...to create rich, umami flavours: layer ingredients, such as miso paste, nutritional yeast, maple syrup, sugar, molasses, smoked paprika, sage, soy, cinnamon, coffee and dark chocolate.
Deep, Dark & Smoky Chilli (page 32)

...to create a speedy ragu: use ready-to-eat or pre-cooked ingredients such as jarred artichokes, roasted peppers and sun-dried tomatoes, that combine to give a rich, slow-cooked flavour.
Henry's 30 Minute Lasagne (page 62)

...to make quick garlic breads: use a speedy garlic and oil sauce.
Ivory Coast Squash & Peanut Stew (page 44)

...for instant caramel flavour: just add Biscoff spread for a quick burst of caramel in dessert dishes.
Coffee Caramel Tearer Sharer (page 218)
Rice Krispie Donuts (page 211)

...for instant spice: use a selection of your favourite hot sauces to give instant spicy flavour to dishes. We like sriracha and Tabasco for quick, fiery hits.

Use packs of pre-cooked...

...rice: to get a meal on the table quickly and easily.
Cauliflower Schnitzel – 3 Ways (page 39)
Butter Tofu Curry (page 105)
Sticky Sichuan Tofu (page 130)
Luxurious Rice Pilaf (page 109)
Roasted Thai Broccoli (page 179)

...lentils: to get your high-protein, high-fibre lentils onto a plate in minutes.
Aubergine & Lentil Meatball Pasta (page 30)
Green Shepherd's Pie (page 58)
Deep, Dark & Smoky Chilli (page 32)

...beans & lentils: to create a delicious, flavourful dal curry in no time at all.
Cheat's Black Dal (page 115)

...beetroot: to get the delicious colour and flavour of beetroot onto your plate instantly.
Beetroot Falafel (page 172)

Use pre-prepped ingredients...

...to save time chopping: use pre-chopped, frozen ingredients, like herbs, sliced onions, diced or sliced peppers, diced squash and other vegetables.
Speedy Restaurant Ramen (page 97)
Salt & Pepper Tofu (page 186)
Taco Salad (page 192)

Plant protein and alternatives

Use veggie sausages: you can mash or blend up veggie sausages to make quick meatballs or a mince.
Super-Meaty Spag Bol (page 84)
Luxurious Rice Pilaf (page 109)

Use plant-based chicken or fish chunks: make a delicious, filling dish without fuss.
Quick Tandoori Kebabs (page 110)
Tartare Sauce Fysh Tacos (page 153)
Happy Chick'n Parmo (page 61)

Work with jackfruit: create pulled jackfruit dishes by draining it, coating it in a spice rub or paste, then oven-baking it.
Moroccan Jackfruit Stew (page 66)
Got-No-Beef Rendang (page 98)
Jackfruit Rendang Burger (page 101)
Jackfruit Shawarma (page 106)

Make tofu crispy: coat it in cornflour (or a gluten-free version) and shallow fry. If you're still waiting to be convinced on tofu, this will convert you.
Butter Tofu Curry page 105)
Sticky Sichuan Tofu (page 130)
Salt & Pepper Tofu (page 186)
Speedy Laksa (page 126)

Use tofu to thicken sauces: silken tofu can create a thick cream, which goes well with savoury dishes as well as sweet.
Creamy Lime Pie (page 224)
Portuguese Custard Tarts (page 229)

Cook with tempeh: build a hearty, protein-rich dish around blanched or steamed tempeh, tofu's older, more refined cousin.
BBQ Tempeh Ribs (page 139)
Theasby's Tempeh Toastie (page 86)
Teriyaki Tempeh (page 196)

Speedy feasts

Sometimes one dish isn't enough and you want to cook a delicious spread. At other times, you may be watching your waistline or trying to keep an eye on the pennies. Let us point you in the right direction with these themed recipe collections, for whatever it is you're after.

BOSH! classics, faster

Our classic dishes – your go-to recipes – faster

- Deep, Dark & Smoky Chilli (page 32)
- Henry's 30 Minute Lasagne (page 62)
- Super-Meaty Spag Bol (page 84)
- Ultimate Vegan Mac & Cheese (page 88)
- Beetroot & Lentil Burger (page 102)
- Butter Tofu Curry (page 105)
- Speedy Pizza – 3 Ways (page 159)
- Berry Buckwheat Pancake Stack (page 261)
- Breakfast Hash Tacos (page 262)

Eating on a budget

Looking to save some cash? Cook these bad boys.

Butternut Squash Carbonara with Crispy Sage (page 51)
Salsa Gnocchi (page 83)
Frying Pan Samosa Pie (page 48)

Eat the rainbow

Want to make sure you're getting enough colour and greens in? You need these.

Rainbow Falafel (page 170)
Taco Salad (page 192)
Winter Roots Salad (page 198)
Quick Mezze Platter (page 142)

Eating for the gym

Higher protein, healthier dishes that are great for gym buffs.

High-carb, low-fat deliciousness

This is low-oil, low-fat, super healthy food.

Perfect for meal prepping

A selection of meals that are easy to prep together for the week to come.

A dinner party to impress

Are your family or friends coming round and you want to put on a tasty dinner party in a hurry? Cook one of these spreads.

Winter Menu

Summer Menu

Make tofu taste amazing

Are you, or is someone in your family, not into tofu? Here are our best tofu choices that'll turn tofu-haters into tofu-lovers.

Ultimate street food

These will make you feel as though you're at a vegan street-food festival with music blaring and a drink in hand.

Storecupboard wonders

Looking to make meals with what you've got in your cupboards? Look no further!

Hearty

01

Cheat's Toad in the Hole with Curry Gravy

Our childhoods were packed with fond memories of our secondary school, High Storrs, where they cooked delicious school dinners. Toad in the hole was a classic lunch for us back then, oop North in Yorkshire. So when we met a BOSH! fan who shared their beloved hack for this dish, using puff pastry instead of Yorkshire pudding, we had to try it. To that person (you know who you are) thanks for the idea, it's an incredible dish!

Serves 3–4

1 x 320g sheet ready-rolled
    dairy-free puff pastry
6 plant-based sausages
2 tbsp unsweetened plant-based milk
1 tbsp curry powder
salt and black pepper

For the curry gravy
2 tbsp vegetable oil
1 red onion
2 garlic cloves
1½ tsp cornflour
250ml boiling water
1 tbsp ketchup
1 tsp English mustard
1 tsp soy sauce
1 tsp nutritional yeast
1 tsp curry powder
handful of fresh coriander
salt and black pepper

To serve
mango chutney

Preheat oven to 200°C • Baking tray • Pastry brush • Frying pan on a medium heat • Kettle boiled

Prepare the toad in the hole • Unroll the pastry and place it on its sheet on the baking tray • Lay the sausages on top and score the pastry either side of each sausage with a sharp knife • In a bowl, mix the milk together with the curry powder and a generous grinding of salt and pepper • Brush the milk mixture over the pastry • Bake on the top shelf of the hot oven for 15 minutes

Meanwhile, make the curry gravy • Add the oil to the hot frying pan • Peel and finely slice the onion and add it to the pan • Peel the garlic cloves and add them to the pan • Cook for 5 minutes, stirring occasionally • Stir in the cornflour to coat the onions and garlic • Add the boiling water, ketchup, mustard, soy sauce, nutritional yeast and curry powder • Stir to combine • Finely slice the coriander stalks, reserving the leaves, and add them to the pan • Stir and then bring to a simmer • Season to taste • Remove and discard the garlic cloves • Add more water if the gravy looks too thick

Serve • Pour the gravy into a jug • Scatter the reserved coriander leaves over the toad in the hole and serve it with the gravy and some mango chutney on the side

Aubergine & Lentil Meatball Pasta

A wonderful and inventive pasta dish offering a new twist on spaghetti, this one uses shop-bought baba ganoush (made with aubergines) to bind the meatballs together, providing an earthy, creamy flavour. There are a lot of heavily processed plant-based 'meatballs' out there nowadays, but making your own is a lot more fun than bunging shop-bought ones in the oven and they're healthier, too!

Serves 4–6

400g spaghetti

For the meatballs
4 sun-dried tomatoes, plus
    2 tbsp oil from the jar
1 x 250g pouch pre-cooked
    puy lentils
75g fresh breadcrumbs
50g pine nuts
10g fresh mint leaves
10g fresh parsley leaves
4 tbsp store-bought baba ganoush
2 tbsp olive oil, for coating
salt and black pepper

For the sauce
2 tbsp olive oil
1 garlic clove
1 tbsp dried oregano
1 x 680g jar passata
1 tbsp balsamic vinegar
salt and black pepper

To serve
olive oil, for drizzling
fresh mint leaves
fresh parsley leaves

Preheat oven to 200°C • **Large saucepan of salted water on a high heat** • **Food processor** • **Line a baking tray** • **Large frying pan** • **Microplane or fine grater** • **Tongs**

Bring the pan of salted water to the boil • Add the spaghetti and cook until al dente, following the instructions on the packet

Meanwhile, make the meatballs • Put all the ingredients for the meatballs, except the olive oil for coating, in the food processor • Blitz to a coarse paste • Taste and season with salt and pepper • Use your hands to roll the mixture into about 20 balls, then toss them in the 2 tablespoons olive oil and place them on the lined baking tray • Bake in the hot oven for 12 minutes, turning them halfway

Make the sauce • Put the frying pan on a medium-high heat • Add the olive oil • Peel and grate the garlic directly into the pan • Add the dried oregano • As soon as the garlic begins to colour, tip in the passata followed by the balsamic vinegar • Allow to bubble away, reducing the heat a little if it starts to boil too much • Season to taste with salt and pepper

Combine • Once the pasta is cooked, use tongs to slosh it into the frying pan with the sauce, taking some of the cooking water with it • Season well with salt and pepper and remove from the heat • Tip in the meatballs and toss gently so you don't break them up •

Serve • Spoon the pasta and meatballs into bowls • Drizzle with a little olive oil and scatter with some more mint and parsley leaves

Deep, Dark & Smoky Chilli

A chilli usually takes a lot of time to cook because it needs to bubble away for ages to achieve a lovely deep flavour. The coffee and molasses in this recipe give it a wonderful richness that you wouldn't expect to achieve in such a short space of time. Next time you're after a warming, hearty meal but you're short on time, give this a whirl! This dish is one of our classics, re-imagined to make it super speedy!

Serves 6

2 tbsp vegetable oil
1 onion
1 tbsp fajita seasoning
1 x 400g tin haricot beans
1 x 400g tin kidney beans
1 x 250g pouch pre-cooked
    Puy lentils
1 x 400g tin chopped tomatoes
1 tsp lazy garlic
1 whole dried ancho or
    other large dried chilli
1 tbsp instant coffee
1 tbsp nutritional yeast
1 tbsp dark brown sugar
200ml boiling water
1 cinnamon stick
2 bay leaves
1 tsp salt

For the quick guac
3 ripe avocados
6 spring onions
handful of fresh coriander leaves
1 tbsp jalapeños from a jar
1 lime
pinch of salt
1 tbsp extra-virgin olive oil

Large frying pan on a medium heat • Kettle boiled • Microplane or fine grater • Normal grater

Make the chilli • Heat the oil in the hot frying pan • Peel and slice the onion and add it to the pan • Add the fajita seasoning and stir to coat the onions • Fry for a few minutes • Tip in the beans, lentils, tomatoes and garlic and stir • Cut a slit in the chilli and put it in a mug with the coffee, nutritional yeast and sugar • Add the boiling water • Stir and tip into the pan • Add the cinnamon stick, bay leaves and salt • Leave to bubble away for 15–20 minutes while you prepare the accompaniments, stirring occasionally and topping up with a little more water if needed

Make the quick guac • Cut the avocados in half, carefully remove the stone and scoop the flesh into a serving bowl • Roughly chop the spring onions, coriander and jalapeños and add to the bowl • Zest and juice the lime and add them to the bowl along with the salt • Roughly run your knife through everything and then mash gently with a fork, but keep the mixture slightly chunky and textured • Drizzle with the olive oil

For the speedy sour cream
1 lime
4 tbsp dairy-free cream cheese
pinch of salt

For the instant salsa
200g cherry tomatoes
    (mixed colours look great)
½ lime
handful of coriander stalks
½ tsp lazy garlic or ½ garlic
    clove, crushed
pinch of salt

To serve
200g dairy-free cheese
1 little gem lettuce
½ red cabbage
½ lime
pinch of salt
18 soft tortillas or taco shells

Make the speedy sour cream • Zest and juice the lime and add to a small bowl • Add the cream cheese and salt and stir with a fork until smooth

Make the instant salsa • Halve the tomatoes and put them in a serving bowl • Juice the lime • Finely chop the coriander stalks and stir them into the tomatoes with the garlic, salt and lime juice

To serve • Grate the cheese into a bowl and take to the table with the guac, sour cream and salsa • Slice the lettuce and red cabbage and put them in a serving bowl • Squeeze over the juice of the lime, add the salt and toss through • Give everyone a plate piled with tacos • Finally, bring the chilli to the table in the pan and let everyone get stuck in!

Black Olive Pesto Pasta

Pesto pasta is easy, delicious and really filling – the perfect speedy dinner. The black olive pesto we've developed for this dish is full of deep, interesting flavours and the breadcrumbs add an amazing crunch. And to top that off, it's effortlessly simple to cook. We use spaghetti, but feel free to use any shape of pasta you have in your cupboard. Happy cooking!

Serves 4

400g spaghetti
drizzle of olive oil
salt and black pepper

For the oregano breadcrumbs
1 piece white bread
1 tsp dried oregano
1 tbsp olive oil

For the black olive pesto
½ small bunch fresh basil
½ small bunch fresh parsley
220g pitted black olives
    (we used Kalamata)
50g almonds
4 tbsp olive oil
1½ tbsp tomato purée
1½ tbsp balsamic vinegar
pinch of salt
pinch of black pepper

Large saucepan of salted water on a high heat • Food processor • Large frying pan • Tongs

Cook the pasta • Bring the pan of salted water to the boil • Add the pasta and cook for 1 minute less than stated on the packet instructions

Meanwhile, make the breadcrumbs • Blitz the bread to coarse breadcrumbs in a food processor • Tip the crumbs into the frying pan along with the dried oregano • Add the olive oil and stir until the crumbs are coated • Put the pan over a medium heat and toast until the breadcrumbs are golden and crisp • Tip into a small bowl and set aside, keeping the frying pan handy

Make the pesto • Reserve a few herbs for garnish and put the rest into the food processor • Blitz together with all the other pesto ingredients until well combined but not completely smooth

Combine • Once the pasta is cooked, put the frying pan over a medium-high heat • Add the pesto to the hot pan with a ladleful of the pasta water • Use tongs to transfer the pasta directly from the saucepan into the frying pan and toss until the pasta is coated with the pesto sauce • Taste and season with salt and pepper

Serve • Swirl the pasta into bowls • Top with a drizzle of olive oil and the oregano breadcrumbs • Scatter with the reserved herbs

Cauliflower Schnitzel – 3 Ways

Cauliflower is such a wonderfully diverse vegetable. You can blitz it and turn it into rice; break it, bake it and use it as a replacement for chicken wings; whizz it into a creamy sauce; or slice it, cover it in breadcrumbs and turn it into schnitzel! We like cauli schnitzel so much we decided to show you three ways to serve it. This is a seriously surprising recipe, with our cornflour cauliflower crisping technique providing the perfect substantial steak. Get big cauliflowers as the larger the stem of the cauli, the fatter the steak.

Original Schnitzel with Slaw & Fries

Serves 2

1 large cauliflower
70g fresh breadcrumbs
50g cornflour
150ml unsweetened plant-based milk
salt and black pepper
vegetable oil, for frying

For the fries
250g oven-bake fries

For the coleslaw
¼ red cabbage
1 carrot
½ green apple
3 tbsp dairy-free mayonnaise
  (or plant-based yoghurt,
  if you prefer)
1 tsp English mustard
salt and black pepper

Preheat oven to 220°C • Baking tray • Microwaveable plate • Clingfilm • Microwave • Large frying pan • Line a large plate with kitchen paper • Grater

Bake the fries • Tip the fries onto a baking tray and cook in the oven according to the packet instructions

Prepare the cauliflower steaks • Pull the leaves from the cauliflower • Holding it upside-down, make 3 slices through the base, 2cm apart, to give you 2 cauliflower steaks • Save the rest of the cauliflower to use another time • Place the steaks on a microwaveable plate, cover with clingfilm and microwave on high for 2 minutes

Heat the oil for frying • Pour a 1cm depth of vegetable oil into the frying pan and place over a medium-high heat

Coat the cauliflower • Tip the breadcrumbs, cornflour and plant-based milk into 3 separate bowls • Season the flour with a big pinch of salt and pepper • Take each of the cauliflower steaks and dip them first into the flour, then into the milk and finally into the breadcrumbs, pressing them onto the cauliflower

Fry the schnitzels • Once the oil is hot, add the cauliflower steaks and fry for 2–3 minutes on each side until golden and cooked through • Transfer to the plate lined with kitchen paper to drain

Make the coleslaw • Finely slice the red cabbage and put it in a bowl • Grate the carrot and apple into the bowl • Add the mayonnaise and mustard, season with salt and pepper and stir well to combine

To serve • Bring the schnitzels to the table and serve with the coleslaw and fries

ORIGINAL
SCHNITZEL WITH
SLAW & FRIES

PAPRIKA SCHNITZEL WITH
MASH & WATERCRESS

GOCHUJANG
SCHNITZEL WITH
RICE & KIMCHI

Gochujang Schnitzel with Rice & Kimchi

Serves 2

1 large cauliflower
70g fresh breadcrumbs
50g cornflour
150ml unsweetened plant-based milk
salt and black pepper
vegetable oil, for frying

For the rice
130g basmati rice
250ml boiling water
2 tbsp sesame seeds
3 spring onions

For the sauce
2 garlic cloves
thumb-sized piece of fresh ginger
2 tbsp dark brown sugar
2 tbsp gochujang paste
    (or sriracha sauce)
2 tbsp soy sauce
2 tsp sesame oil

To serve
2 tbsp vegan kimchi

Kettle boiled • Microwaveable plate • Clingfilm• Microwave • Microwaveable bowl • Clean tea towel • Large frying pan • Line a plate with kitchen paper • Microplane or fine grater • Small saucepan

Prepare the cauliflower steaks • Pull the leaves from the cauliflower • Holding it upside-down, make 3 slices through the base, 2cm apart, to give you 2 cauliflower steaks • Save the rest of the cauliflower to use another time • Place the steaks on the microwaveable plate, cover with clingfilm and microwave on high for 2 minutes

Cook the rice • Rinse the rice well, then tip it into the microwaveable bowl • Pour in the boiling water and microwave on high for 8 minutes • Cover with the clean tea towel and set aside

Heat the oil for frying • Pour a 1cm depth of oil into the large frying pan and place over a medium-high heat

Coat the cauliflower • Tip the breadcrumbs, cornflour and milk into 3 separate bowls • Season the flour with a big pinch of salt and pepper • Take each of the cauliflower steaks and dip them first into the flour, then into the milk and finally into the breadcrumbs, pressing them onto the cauliflower

Fry the schnitzels • Once the oil is hot, add the cauliflower steaks and fry for 2–3 minutes on each side until golden and cooked through • Transfer to the plate lined with kitchen paper to drain

Make the sauce • Peel the garlic • Grate the garlic and ginger directly into the small saucepan • Add the remaining sauce ingredients and set the pan over a medium heat • Simmer for 3–4 minutes until the sauce is syrupy • Remove from the heat and set aside

Use a fork to fluff up the rice • Season with salt and pepper • Stir through the sesame seeds, reserving a few for garnish • Slice the spring onions and stir them through as well

Serve • Drizzle the schnitzels with the sauce and serve alongside the rice with a sprinkling of sesame seeds and a spoonful of kimchi

Paprika Schnitzel with Mash & Watercress

Serves 2

1 large cauliflower
70g fresh breadcrumbs
50g cornflour
150ml unsweetened plant-based milk
salt and black pepper
vegetable oil, for frying

For the potatoes
400g baby potatoes
50ml unsweetened plant-based milk
salt and black pepper

For the paprika sauce
1 tbsp olive oil
½ onion
1 garlic clove
1½ tsp paprika
2 fresh thyme sprigs
100ml oat cream
150ml vegetable stock
1 lemon
salt and black pepper

For the watercress salad
70g watercress
2 tbsp olive oil
1 lemon
salt and black pepper

Kettle boiled • Large saucepan with a lid • Microwaveable plate • Clingfilm • Microwave • 1 medium and 1 large frying pan • Line a plate with kitchen paper • Microplane or fine grater • Whisk • Masher

Start with the potatoes • Tip them into the saucepan and cover them with boiling water • Add a big pinch of salt • Cover, bring to the boil and cook for 15 minutes until completely soft

Prepare the cauliflower steaks • Pull the leaves from the cauliflower • Holding it upside-down, make 3 slices through the base, 2cm apart, to give you 2 steaks • Save the rest of the cauliflower to use another time • Place the steaks on the microwaveable plate, cover with clingfilm and microwave on high for 2 minutes

Start the sauce • Pour the olive oil into the medium frying pan and place over a medium-high heat • Finely chop the onion and add it to the pan with a big pinch of salt • Fry for 5 minutes • Pour a 1cm depth of oil into the large frying pan and place it over a medium-high heat

Coat the cauliflower • Tip the breadcrumbs, cornflour and milk into 3 separate bowls • Season the flour with a big pinch of salt and pepper • Take each of the cauliflower steaks and dip them first into the flour, then into the milk and finally into the breadcrumbs, pressing them onto the cauliflower

Fry the schnitzels • Once the oil is hot, add the cauliflower steaks to the large frying pan • Fry for 2–3 minutes on each side until golden and cooked through • Transfer to the plate lined with kitchen paper

Finish the sauce • Peel the garlic and grate it directly into the medium frying pan over the onions • Stir in the paprika • Pick the leaves from the thyme and add them to the pan • Pour the oat cream and stock into a bowl and whisk to combine • Add to the pan • Squeeze in the juice from one of the lemons • Bring to the boil, season with salt and pepper, then reduce the heat to low and leave to bubble away

Return to the mash • Drain the potatoes, then return them to the pan and pour in the plant-based milk • Mash and season with plenty of salt and pepper

Prepare the salad • Add the watercress and olive oil to a bowl • Halve the lemon and squeeze in the juice • Toss to combine • Season well and add more lemon juice if required

Serve • Drizzle the schnitzels with the paprika sauce • Serve with the mash and watercress salad alongside

Ivory Coast Squash & Peanut Stew

There are variations of this stew all across West Africa, but this one, laden with deliciously sweet butternut squash, is inspired by the version that is specific to the Ivory Coast. Squash can take quite a bit of work and time to prepare, but here we have taken away the faff by using a food processor. Make this recipe and you'll have a rich, silky stew that's super healthy, really filling and packed full of flavour. Yum!

Serves 4

1 onion
500g butternut squash
1 fresh red chilli
1 tbsp coconut oil
1 tsp lazy garlic or 1 garlic clove,
    crushed
1 tbsp nutritional yeast
½ tsp coriander seeds
½ tsp ground cinnamon
½ tsp ground allspice
large thumb-sized piece
    of fresh ginger
1 tbsp smooth peanut butter
1 x 400g tin chickpeas
500ml vegetable stock
4 large handfuls of greens (kale,
    cavolo nero or spinach)
½ orange
1 tsp salt
dash of apple cider vinegar

For the garlic chapatis
4 chapatis
1 tbsp coconut oil
½ tsp lazy garlic or ½ garlic
    clove, crushed

For the crunchy peanut sprinkle
handful of fresh coriander
    (leaves and stems)
pinch of salt
large handful of roasted peanuts

Preheat grill to max • Food processor • Large frying pan with lid • Microplane or fine grater • Kettle boiled • Small saucepan • Pestle and mortar (optional)

Prepare the veg • Peel and roughly chop the onion • Halve the squash, remove any seeds and roughly chop – no need to peel • Remove the stem from the chilli but keep the seeds (unless you prefer things milder!) • Place the onion, squash and chilli into a large food processor and pulse until chopped into very small chunks

Make the stew • Heat the coconut oil in the large frying pan over a medium heat • Add the chopped veg and stir to coat • Add the garlic and yeast • Lightly crush the coriander seeds and add them to the pan along with the other spices • Stir well • Grate the ginger directly into the pan • Spoon in the peanut butter • Drain the chickpeas, then add to the pan along with the stock and stir again • Reduce the heat to low, cover and leave to simmer for 15 minutes

Make the garlic chapatis • Heat the chapatis under the hot grill • Meanwhile, put the small pan over a medium heat • Melt the coconut oil and then add the garlic • Brush the bread with the garlic oil • Return the chapatis to the grill to keep warm, but turn off the heat

Finish the stew • Prepare the greens by removing any tough stems • Zest and juice the orange and set the zest aside • Add the greens, orange juice, salt and vinegar to the stew • Stir, then leave to cook uncovered for 3–4 minutes, until reduced and thickened

Make the crunchy peanut sprinkle • Roughly chop the coriander and add to a small bowl with the reserved orange zest and salt • Roughly bash the peanuts in the pestle and mortar (or roughly chop them) and tip them into the bowl • Stir to combine

Serve • Spoon the stew into bowls and top with the peanut sprinkle • Serve with the garlic chapatis, cut into triangles, for scooping

Robinson's Rarebit

Cheese on toast's more sophisticated cousin, Welsh rarebit gives all the comfort of its popular relative, but adds an undercurrent of mellow spice from the mustard and Henderson's relish. The delicious cheesy sauce sits on a bed of crispy pan-fried leeks, which in turn sit astride a slice of freshly toasted sourdough. As perfected with the help of our buddy and super-talented chef Luke Robinson, who we've known since we were little nippers. Simple, but absolutely delicious.

Serves 4

30g plant-based butter
30g plain flour
150ml lager or pale ale
150g smoked dairy-free cheese
1 tbsp Henderson's Relish
    (or vegan Worcestershire sauce/
    mushroom ketchup)
1 tsp mustard
1 large leek
1 tbsp light olive oil
4 slices crusty sourdough
    or granary bread
drizzle of extra-virgin olive oil

To serve
handful of flat-leaf parsley leaves
handful of watercress
pinch of cayenne pepper
    or hot sauce

Preheat grill to high • Small saucepan on a medium heat • Whisk • Grater • Large heavy-based frying pan with a lid

Make the topping • Put the butter in the hot saucepan • Tip in the flour and stir vigorously with the whisk to form a roux • Add the lager or pale ale, a few tablespoons at a time, whisking constantly until incorporated and smooth • Grate in the cheese using the largest holes • Add the Henderson's Relish and mustard and stir everything together for 1 minute until fully combined • Remove from the heat

Fry the leek • Thinly slice the leek • Put the frying pan over a medium-high heat • Pour in the light olive oil • Add the leek to the hot oil and fry for about 6 minutes, stirring occasionally, until softened and lightly browned • Cover the pan for the last 2 minutes to help soften the leeks

To finish • Lightly toast the bread on both sides under the grill • Divide the leeks between the slices • Pour the topping over each slice and drizzle with extra-virgin olive oil • Return to the grill for 1–3 minutes, until the topping is lightly golden or even starting to blacken a bit

Serve • Chop the fresh parsley and sprinkle over the rarebits • Serve with the watercress and a pinch of cayenne pepper or some hot sauce

Frying Pan Samosa Pie

This dish has all the flavours of our favourite Indian snack in a giant pie. What's not to like? Seriously. Potato, cauliflower and peas form the main bulk of the filling and the spice profile is simple, familiar and very effective. The top of the pie is made from crispy, crunchy, shop-bought filo pastry, which makes this pie look as good as it tastes. If you like samosas, you need to give this a go!

Serves 4

6 sheets filo pastry
vegetable oil, for brushing
nigella seeds, for sprinkling

For the filling
2 baking potatoes
1 small cauliflower (or
    ½ large cauliflower)
1 tbsp vegetable oil
1 fresh green chilli
2 garlic cloves
thumb-sized piece of fresh ginger
1 tbsp curry powder
2 tsp ground turmeric
1 tsp fennel seeds
350ml vegetable stock
175g frozen peas
small bunch of fresh coriander
1 lime
salt and black pepper

To serve
coconut yoghurt

Preheat oven to 200°C • Large microwaveable bowl • Clingfilm • Microwave • Pastry brush • Baking tray • Large frying pan with lid • Microplane or fine grater

Cook the potatoes • Peel and roughly chop the potatoes into 2cm chunks • Tip into a large microwaveable bowl and cover with clingfilm • Microwave on high for 4–6 minutes

Cook the cauliflower • Roughly chop the cauliflower florets into bite-sized chunks • Add to the bowl with the partially cooked potatoes and microwave for a further 6 minutes

Meanwhile, bake the pastry • Take one sheet of filo and brush it with vegetable oil, then sprinkle with nigella seeds • Scrunch it up and place it on the baking tray • Repeat with the rest of the pastry • Bake in the oven for 6–8 minutes until golden, keeping an eye on them – they can turn from golden to brown very quickly!

Make the filling • Add the tablespoon of vegetable oil to the frying pan and place it over a high heat • Chop the green chilli, removing the seeds if you don't like too much heat • Peel the garlic • Grate the garlic and ginger directly into the pan • Add the green chilli to the pan along with a pinch of salt • Add the curry powder, turmeric and fennel seeds, then tip in the cooked cauliflower and potato chunks • Stir to coat in the spices • Add the stock and season well • Cover the pan and cook for 2–3 minutes • Take off the lid and use a fork or potato masher to lightly smush the mixture • Add the peas to the pan and cook for 2 minutes, then remove from the heat • Roughly chop the coriander and stir it through the mixture • Halve the lime and squeeze in the juice, then stir it through

Assemble • Top the frying pan with the filo scrunches and bring it to the table • Serve straight from the pan with a spoonful of coconut yoghurt

Butternut Squash Carbonara with Crispy Sage

Butternut squash has such a beautiful natural flavour and in this recipe we let that flavour take centre stage. The sauce is great on its own but the crispy aromatic sage complements the squash perfectly. It will also make your kitchen smell incredible! Thick, creamy and wonderfully unctuous, this is real comfort food that will put smiles on the faces of your whole family.

Serves 4

380g butternut squash or pumpkin
50g cashew nuts
3–4 tbsp olive oil, plus extra
    for drizzling
small bunch of fresh sage
400g spaghetti

For the sauce
1 onion
2 garlic cloves
1 vegetable stock cube
4 tbsp nutritional yeast
salt and black pepper

Large saucepan of salted water on a high heat • Microwaveable bowl • Clingfilm • Microwave • Large frying pan • Line a plate with kitchen paper • Microplane or fine grater • Food processor

Microwave the squash • Peel and cut the squash into 1½ cm cubes • Tip the squash and cashew nuts into a microwaveable bowl, cover with clingfilm and microwave on high for 5 minutes

Make the crispy sage • Pour the oil into the large frying pan and set over a high heat • Pick the sage leaves and fry them in the hot oil until dark green and crisp • Remove and drain on the plate lined with kitchen paper • Keep the pan and oil for making the sauce

Cook the pasta • Add the spaghetti to the pan of boiling salted water • Cook for 1 minute less than stated on the packet instructions

Meanwhile, make the sauce • Peel and finely chop the onion • Put the frying pan back on a medium heat • Add the onion to the hot pan and fry for 3–4 minutes • Peel the garlic and grate it directly into the pan • Fry for 2 minutes • Tip the microwaved squash and cashews into the pan and cook for 1 minute • Add a large ladle or mugful of the pasta water to the pan along with the vegetable stock cube • Stir until the cube has dissolved, then tip the contents of the pan into a food processor • Add the nutritional yeast and a generous sprinkling of salt and pepper • Blitz to a smooth sauce, adding a little more pasta water to loosen, if necessary

Combine • Put the frying pan over a medium heat and pour in the sauce • Transfer the cooked spaghetti into the sauce, taking a little of the cooking water with it • Toss until the sauce is silky and coats the pasta • Add a splash more pasta water if it looks at all claggy

Serve • Twirl the pasta into bowls • Top with the crispy sage, a drizzle of olive oil and some black pepper

Thanksgiving Roast

We love a good roast, at Thanksgiving, or really any time! There's something really special about sitting around a table with our nearest and dearest to give thanks for all of the good things in our lives. This celebratory menu is a feast of delicious autumnal flavours and, if you're organised, can be on the table in 30 minutes flat, leaving you with more time to spend with your friends and family. There's quite a lot going on here, so be sure to get all your trays, pans and ingredients ready before you start!

Serves 4

90g plant-based butter

For the Sweet Potato & Pecan Pie
2 sweet potatoes
pinch of salt
1 tbsp oat milk
50g oats
20g demerara sugar
40g pecans

For the Maple-Roasted Roots
2 carrots
2 parsnips
2 tbsp olive oil
1 tbsp maple syrup
handful of fresh thyme leaves
1 lemon
salt and black pepper

For the Buttered Corn & Parsley
1 x 165g tin sweetcorn
whole or grated nutmeg
handful of flat-leaf parsley

Preheat oven to max • Line a baking tray • Kettle boiled • Large saucepan with a lid • Steamer or colander • 2 small saucepans • Microplane or fine grater • Small baking dish or roasting tin • Large bowl • Frying pan • Line a plate with kitchen paper

For the Sweet Potato & Pecan Pie • Peel and cube the sweet potatoes • Place in the saucepan, cover with boiling water, add some salt and set over a medium heat for 10 minutes • Place the steamer or colander on top ready for the other roots

Melt the plant-based butter in a small saucepan and set aside

For the Maple-Roasted Roots • Peel the carrots and parsnips, if necessary, then quarter or half lengthways if small, or cut into thin batons • Place in the steamer, put the lid on and steam for 5 minutes • Remove and spread over the lined baking tray • Cover with the 2 tablespoons olive oil and the maple syrup • Pick the thyme leaves, if the stems are woody, and halve the lemon • Sprinkle the thyme over the veg and drizzle with a squeeze of the lemon • Taste and season with salt and pepper • Place on the top shelf of the hot oven to roast for 15 minutes

For the Buttered Corn & Parsley • Put the other small saucepan over a low heat • Empty the sweetcorn into the pan with a third of the melted butter • Add a grating of nutmeg • Heat on low for 10 minutes, stirring occasionally

Return to the Sweet Potato Pie • After 10 minutes the sweet potato should be very soft • Drain well and return to the pan • Add the oat milk and salt and mash until smooth • Taste and season with more salt if necessary • Scoop into the baking dish or roasting tin • In a bowl, mix together the oats, sugar and pecans with a third of the melted butter and tip over the top of the mash • Place in the hot oven next to the root veg

For the Red Cabbage
& Cranberry Dressing
1 tbsp soy sauce
1 tbsp red wine vinegar
1 tbsp cranberry sauce
1 tbsp olive oil
¼ red cabbage

For the pan-fried seitan
1 tsp dried oregano
300g seitan steaks
80g vegan 'bacon' rashers (optional)

For the greens
drizzle of olive oil
2 large handfuls of collard greens,
    kale or spring greens
½ orange
dash of red wine vinegar
whole or ground nutmeg
salt and black pepper

To serve
instant vegan gravy
cranberry sauce

For the Red Cabbage & Cranberry Dressing • Place all the dressing ingredients in the bottom of the bowl you will use to serve the cabbage and whisk together • Finely shred the cabbage and tip it into the bowl • Toss to coat

For the pan-fried seitan • Place the frying pan over a medium heat • Add the final third of the melted butter and add the dried oregano • Once the herbs are sizzling, add the seitan and vegan 'bacon' rashers, if using, and fry lightly on both sides • Remove and set aside to drain on kitchen paper • Return the pan to the heat

For the greens • Drizzle some olive oil into the pan • Trim the greens and add them to the pan • Increase the heat to high and squeeze over the juice of the orange and the red wine vinegar • Fry for a few minutes, then add a grating of nutmeg and season with salt and pepper • Take the pan to the table

To serve • Make the gravy according to packet instructions • Check on the roasted veg and the pie and, if not browned to your liking, pop under the grill for a couple of minutes • Add a handful of parsley leaves to the corn and take it to the table with the other dishes, the gravy and the cranberry sauce • Carefully remove the root veg and pie from under the grill and take them to the table •
Let everyone dig in and give thanks!

Lemon, Courgette & Crispy Caper Pasta

This dish is like an exercise in simplicity, bringing a few delicious and complementary flavours together and pairing with perfectly cooked pasta shells. Crispy capers are a revelation in this one and taste just as good on their own as in the pasta! All the flavours and wonderful green colours in this dish make it an incredibly tasty, healthy and gorgeous-looking meal.

Serves 2

200g pasta shells
2 courgettes
small handful of fresh mint leaves
small handful of fresh dill
1–2 lemons
1 garlic clove
1 tsp fennel seeds
100g frozen peas
60g capers
1 tbsp olive oil
salt and black pepper

For the crispy capers
2 tbsp olive oil
2 tbsp capers

Large saucepan of salted water on a high heat • Large frying pan on a high heat • Kitchen paper • Microplane or fine grater

Bring the pan of salted water to the boil • Add the pasta and cook until al dente, following the instructions on the packet

Make the crispy capers • Heat the 2 tablespoons olive oil in the hot frying pan • Dry the 2 tablespoons capers with kitchen paper, then tip them into the hot oil • Fry for 2–3 minutes until crisp • Remove to drain on kitchen paper • Keep the pan on the heat

Cook the courgettes • Chop the courgettes into small chunks • Add to the pan with pinch of salt and fry for 7–10 minutes, turning regularly • Roughly chop the herbs • Zest one of the lemons and cut it in half • Peel and grate the garlic directly into the pan • Add the fennel seeds and cook for 2 minutes until the garlic is golden • Add the frozen peas and the 60g capers and cook for 1 minute • Remove from the heat • Add the lemon zest, taste and if you like more lemon, squeeze in the juice from the lemon halves • Add most of the chopped herbs and the tablespoon of olive oil • Season with a big pinch of salt and pepper

To finish • Drain the cooked pasta and transfer it to the pan with the courgettes and peas • Toss well, taste and season if necessary

Serve • Scatter the pasta with the crispy capers and reserved herbs • Zest the second lemon over the top, then cut it into wedges to serve on the side

Green Shepherd's Pie

Shepherd's pie is delicious but making one is usually a long, drawn-out affair. The idea of a speedy version might be music to your ears. This pie is jacked up with loads of protein-packed Puy lentils, nutrient-dense dark greens and, of course, really filling potato. Make this on a chilly autumnal day – it'll really help warm your cockles. Depending on the size of pan you use, you might not need all the mash. If you have any leftover, simply store it in the fridge for later.

Serves 4–6

2 tbsp sunflower oil
2 onions
3 garlic cloves
700g passata
150ml vegetable stock
2 x 250g pouches cooked Puy lentils
1–3 tbsp mushroom ketchup,
    Henderson's Relish or vegan
    Worcestershire Sauce
salt and black pepper

For the mash
1kg fluffy potatoes
6 tbsp extra-virgin olive oil
salt and black pepper

For the green topping
200g cavolo nero
70g pine nuts
50g baby leaf spinach
1 garlic clove
60ml extra-virgin olive oil
½ lemon
salt and black pepper

Large saucepan of salted water on a high heat • Large, wide, flameproof casserole dish or frying pan • Microplane or fine grater • Steamer pan or colander • Frying pan • Food processor

Make the filling • Pour the sunflower oil into the hot casserole or frying pan • Cut the onions into 1cm thick wedges • Add to the pan and cook for 5 minutes, stirring regularly, until browned and lightly charred • Reduce the heat to medium-low • Peel the garlic and grate it directly into the casserole • Stir-fry for 1 minute • Add the passata, stock and lentils, increase the heat and bring to the boil, then reduce to a medium simmer and cook for 10–15 minutes • Add the mushroom ketchup, Henderson's Relish or Worcestershire Sauce to taste, and heat through • Season with salt and pepper

Meanwhile, prepare the veg • Peel and chop the potatoes into 3cm chunks • Add them to the pan of boiling water and simmer, covered, for 8–10 minutes, or until tender • Trim the cavolo nero but keep the leaves long • Place in the steamer pan or colander and set on top of the pan to steam over the potatoes for the last 3 minutes

Make the green topping • Put a frying pan over a medium heat • Sprinkle over the pine nuts and toast until golden • Take off the heat • Transfer the cavolo nero to a food processor along with 2 tablespoons of the potato cooking liquid • Roughly chop the spinach and add to the processor, along with the garlic, olive oil, 50g of the pine nuts and some salt and pepper • Squeeze in lemon juice to taste • Blend until smooth

Mash the potatoes • Drain the potatoes and tip them back into the pan • Mash with the olive oil and some salt and pepper

Assemble the pie • Spread the green sauce over the filling in the casserole • Spread the mash on top • Sprinkle with the reserved toasted pine nuts

Happy Chick'n Parmo

There are many varieties of this dish, from the Italian *parma* to the Teesside parmo, a super-popular dish in the North of England. We've used a shop-bought vegan chicken cutlet to speed things up, and made a really cool speedy béchamel, so you can put together this gourmet (if you can call it that) meal in minutes. Rich, decadent, creamy and moreish, we urge you to try this. It's a super-speedy showstopper!

Serves 2

2 fillets breaded vegan chick'n
20g plant-based parmesan
olive oil, for drizzling

For the tomato sauce
250g passata
1 small onion or shallot
1 tsp lazy garlic or 1 garlic
    clove, crushed
1 tsp dried oregano
1 tsp sugar
1 tbsp extra-virgin olive oil
1 tsp balsamic vinegar
handful of fresh basil leaves
large pinch of salt

For the cheat's béchamel
75ml soya cream
25ml unsweetened plant-based milk
25g plant-based parmesan
25g dairy-free smoked cheese
4 fresh sage leaves (optional)
whole or ground nutmeg
1 tsp nutritional yeast
dash of white wine vinegar
salt and black pepper

For the garlic ciabatta
1 ciabatta
handful of flat-leaf parsley
1 tbsp plant-based butter
pinch of salt
½ tsp lazy garlic or ½ garlic
    clove, crushed

For the rocket salad
2 handfuls of rocket
drizzle of olive oil
½ lemon
dash of balsamic vinegar

Preheat grill to high • Small ovenproof serving dish • 2 saucepans • Grater • Baking tray

Grill the chick'n • Put the vegan chick'n pieces in the ovenproof dish and grill for 5 minutes on each side

Make the tomato sauce • Put a saucepan over a low heat • Add the passata • Peel and halve the onion or shallot and add it to the pan • Add the remaining sauce ingredients, roughly tearing the basil, but leaving a few leaves for garnish • Leave to gently bubble away

Make the cheat's béchamel • Put the second saucepan over a low heat • Add the soya cream and plant-based milk • Grate in the cheeses • Throw in the sage leaves and grate in ½ teaspoon nutmeg • Add the nutritional yeast, white wine vinegar and the salt and pepper • Stir until the cheese melts and the sauce thickens

Meanwhile, make the garlic ciabatta • Slice the ciabatta and place it on the baking tray • Grill on both sides until lightly toasted • Chop the parsley • Put the plant-based butter, garlic, salt and chopped parsley in a small bowl • Spread the toasted breads with the garlic butter

Assemble • Remove the onion or shallot from the tomato sauce and pour the sauce over the chick'n pieces in the dish • Remove the sage leaves from the béchamel and pour it over the top • Grate over the plant-based parmesan and drizzle over a little olive oil • Put back under the grill for a few minutes until brown and bubbling

Meanwhile, make the rocket salad • Put the rocket in a salad bowl • At the last minute, dress directly in the bowl with the olive oil, a squeeze of lemon and the balsamic vinegar • Lightly toss

Serve • Carefully remove the oven dish from the grill • Tear a few more basil leaves over the top to garnish • Serve with the garlic ciabatta and rocket salad

Henry's 30 Minute Lasagne

Lasagne, one of humanity's finest inventions, is a delicious thing but very much a labour of love. It takes hours! So we made – wait for it – a 30-minute lasagne! No joke. It's so fast. If you make one dish from this book, let this be it. The ragu is rich and meaty, the béchamel is deliciously creamy and the top of the lasagne is surprisingly cheesy. No one you make this for will believe you when you tell them how speedy it is to put together.

Serves 4

250g lasagne sheets
50g plant-based parmesan
handful of fresh basil leaves

For the deli ragu
2 garlic cloves
1 tsp smoked paprika
5 sun-dried tomatoes
3 roasted red peppers from a jar
680ml passata
1 tbsp olive oil
220g soya mince
160g grilled artichokes
salt and black pepper

For the cheat's béchamel
200ml plant-based crème fraîche
1 tbsp nutritional yeast
50g plant-based parmesan
salt and black pepper

Preheat grill to high • Large saucepan of salted water on a high heat • Food processor • Large frying pan on a high heat • Microplane or fine grater

Make the ragu • Peel the garlic cloves and add them to the food processor • Add the smoked paprika, sundried tomatoes, red peppers and passata and blitz to combine • Meanwhile, heat the olive oil in the hot frying pan and add the soya mince • Pour over the tomato sauce and season with salt and black pepper • Reduce the heat to medium and let bubble away for 10 minutes, stirring occasionally • Chop the artichokes into small chunks and stir into the sauce

Meanwhile, parboil the lasagne sheets • Bring the pan of salted water to the boil • Snap the lasagne sheets roughly into thirds and add to the boiling water • Boil for 3 minutes then drain and rinse with cold water

Assemble • Tip the lasagne sheets into the ragu and use a spoon to carefully fold them through the sauce, mixing well • Use the spoon to make the top as flat as possible • Remove the frying pan from the heat

Make the cheat's béchamel • Put the crème fraîche and nutritional yeast in a bowl and stir to combine • Grate in the 50g plant-based parmesan and season with salt and pepper

To finish • Tip the béchamel over the top of the ragu and spread it evenly with the back of a spoon • Grate over the remaining plant-based parmesan • Transfer to the hot grill to brown for 5 minutes • Tear the basil leaves over the top and serve

Greens Gratin

This warming dish is topped with a wonderful layer of crispy polenta-coated mushrooms that give way to an unctuous filling of green veg cooked in a nutmeg-flecked creamy sauce. It's the kind of comfort food that cold days are made for – perfect for stoking the fires after a chilly winter walk.

Serves 4

1 tbsp vegetable oil
2 leeks
20g plain flour
100ml oat cream
500ml unsweetened plant-based milk
200g greens (large-leaf spinach,
    or cavolo nero)
whole or ground nutmeg
salt and black pepper

For the crispy mushroom topping
75g walnut halves
4 tbsp vegetable oil
500g mushrooms (we used 150g
    shiitake and 350g portobellini)
3 garlic cloves
60g polenta
few pinches of chilli flakes (optional)
5g dill (optional)
salt and black pepper

Preheat oven to 200°C • Large shallow casserole or large frying pan on a low heat • Whisk • Large non-stick roasting tin • Large mixing bowl

Start with the sauce • Add the vegetable oil to the casserole or frying pan • Thinly slice the leeks, add them to the hot oil and cook for about 6 minutes until softened but not coloured • Put the flour in a jug with the oat cream and whisk together • Add to the pan • Pour in the plant-based milk, mix well and bring to the boil • Reduce to a simmer and cook gently for 8 minutes • Trim and roughly chop the greens, add them to the casserole and cook for 3–4 minutes (2 minutes if you're using large-leaf spinach) • Season with a grating of nutmeg and some salt and pepper

Meanwhile, toast the walnuts • Spread the walnut halves over the roasting tin and dry toast in the hot oven for 5 minutes • Remove, tip onto a chopping board, then set aside • Pour 3 tablespoons of the oil into the roasting tin and put it in the oven to heat up for 5 minutes

Meanwhile, prepare the rest of the topping • Slice any large mushrooms • Peel and crush the garlic cloves • In a large mixing bowl, mix the remaining tablespoon of oil with the mushrooms, garlic, polenta, chilli flakes, if using, and some salt and pepper – use your hands to get them nicely coated • Once the oil in the roasting tin is hot, add the mushroom mixture, toss well and bake for 8 minutes, mixing halfway through

To finish • Chop the dill, if using, and stir most of it into the sauce, reserving some for garnish • Spoon the crispy mushrooms on top of the sauce • Chop the toasted walnuts and sprinkle them over the top • Garnish with the remaining dill, if using

Moroccan Jackfruit Stew

Jackfruit has become increasingly popular in recent years and it's easy to see why. When cooked properly, the texture of tinned jackfruit is extremely meaty and it takes on flavour beautifully. Our video for Moroccan Jackfruit Stew was really popular, so we decided to speedify the recipe for this book. We're positive you won't be disappointed! It's wonderfully fragrant, rich and luxurious – a real crowd-pleaser.

Serves 4

2 tbsp vegetable oil
2 onions
2 tbsp ras el hanout paste
1 tsp paprika
1 tsp ground cinnamon
½ tsp lazy garlic or ½ garlic
    clove, crushed
400g passata or chopped tomatoes
1 x 400g tin chickpeas
80g dried apricots
1 x 400g tin jackfruit
80g pitted black/Kalamata olives
salt and black pepper

For the lemon couscous
200g couscous
1 lemon
salt

To serve
handful of flaked almonds
handful of shelled pistachios
pinch of salt
handful of fresh mint leaves
handful of pomegranate seeds
olive oil, for drizzling

Kettle boiled • Large frying pan or casserole with lid on a medium heat • Tupperware or tub with lid • Pestle and mortar

Make the stew • Add the oil to the hot pan • Peel and finely slice the onions • Add them to the pan with the ras el hanout paste, paprika, cinnamon and garlic • Stir and cook for 5–10 minutes until softened • Pour in the passata and chickpeas with their water and stir • Roughly chop the dried apricots and shred the jackfruit and add them to the pan • Add the olives, stir and taste for seasoning • The stew should be thick, but if it needs a little loosening add a dash of boiling water from the kettle • Cover with the lid and leave to simmer

Make the lemon couscous • Put the couscous into the lidded tub • Zest over the lemon, then halve it and squeeze in the juice of one half • Put the squeezed lemon half in the tub with the couscous and save the other half for later • Pour over enough freshly boiled water to cover the couscous by 5mm, then quickly secure the lid and set aside for 5 minutes

To finish • Bash together the almonds, pistachios and a little salt in a pestle and mortar • Finely chop the mint leaves • Take the lid off the tub of couscous, add a generous pinch of salt and fluff it up with a fork • Squeeze over the juice from the reserved lemon half

To serve • Scoop the couscous into wide serving bowls • Top each with a ladleful of stew • Sprinkle over the pomegranate seeds, crushed nuts and chopped mint • Drizzle with olive oil

Crispy Jacket Potatoes

Jacket potatoes are great but they take ages in the oven. Well, in true speedy fashion, we've hacked them! This way of making jackets uses a microwave and a pan, which is pretty crazy, but it really works. Of course, jacket potatoes are good with vegan cheese, they're good with chickpea 'tuna' and they're good with chilli, but the list of tasty fillings doesn't stop there! We've got three great alternatives for you and you can make all three in one quick cook.

Serves 6

6 small/medium white potatoes
   (about 8.5cm long) or medium
   sweet potatoes (about 10cm long)
   or a mix of both
1 tbsp vegetable oil
salt

For the quick smoky BBQ beans
1 x 400g tin haricot beans
1 tsp lazy garlic or 1 garlic clove, crushed
1 tbsp tomato purée
½ tsp smoked paprika
1 tbsp soy sauce
2 tbsp vegan BBQ sauce
2 thyme sprigs
large pinch of smoked salt

For the herb cheese
100g dairy-free cream cheese
1 tsp lazy garlic or
   1 garlic clove, crushed
½ lemon
handful of fresh chives
olive oil, for drizzling
salt

For the chestnut butter
70g vacuum-packed
   cooked chestnuts
1 tsp maple syrup
1 tbsp water
pinch of salt

For the dressed salad
1 little gem lettuce
50g watercress
2 tbsp olive oil
1 tbsp wholegrain mustard
½ lemon
salt

Microwaveable bowl • Clingfilm • Microwave • Saucepan • Small blender or food processor • 2 large frying pans • Jam jar with a lid

Start with the jackets • Pierce the potatoes with a sharp knife and put them in a microwaveable bowl • Cover with clingfilm and microwave on high for 15 minutes • Meanwhile, make the filling

Make the quick smoky BBQ beans • Add the beans with their liquid to a saucepan over a medium heat • Add all the other ingredients and leave to simmer while you make the other fillings

Make the herb cheese • Put the cream cheese and garlic in a bowl • Squeeze in the lemon juice and mix with a fork • Finely chop the chives and stir them in • Drizzle with olive oil and sprinkle with salt

Make the chestnut butter • Put the chestnuts, maple syrup, water and salt into the blender or food processor and blitz until smooth

Finish the jackets • Put 2 large frying pans over a medium heat and pour half the vegetable oil into each • Take the potatoes out of the microwave and carefully remove the clingfilm • Cut the potatoes in half and add them to the hot frying pans, skin-sides down • Sprinkle each with a generous pinch of salt • Cook, turning occasionally, until crisped up

Make the salad • Separate the lettuce leaves, rinse and shake dry • Add to a salad bowl along with the watercress • Pour the olive oil and mustard into the jam jar • Squeeze in the lemon juice and season to taste with salt • Secure the lid and shake to emulsify • Pour the dressing over the leaves and toss to combine

Serve • Arrange the potatoes on a platter and take it to the table along with the salad bowl and fillings

Lizzie's Lemon & Artichoke Risotto

If you have a taste for citrus and you like risotto, you're definitely going to have to give this a try. And don't just take our word for it! Our friend Lizzie Mayson is the talented photographer responsible for all the pictures in our cookbooks. She's tried every single one of the dishes that have appeared in our books, so when she excitedly proclaimed that this was her favourite recipe in *Speedy Bosh!* we were chuffed.

Serves 2

200g risotto rice
600ml vegetable stock
2 tbsp olive oil
½ onion or 1 shallot
1 garlic clove
1 tsp fennel seeds
125ml white wine
1 x 175g pack chargrilled artichokes
30g hazelnuts
2 small lemons
60g rocket
30g plant-based parmesan (optional)
small bunch of chives
salt and black pepper

Large saucepan with a lid on a medium-high heat • Frying pan on a medium heat • Microplane or fine grater

Get the risotto started • Tip the rice and 300ml of the stock into the hot saucepan • Cover and cook for 5 minutes • Pour 1 tablespoon of the olive oil into the hot frying pan • Finely chop the onion or shallot and add it to the pan along with a big pinch of salt • Fry for 2 minutes • Peel and grate the garlic directly into the pan • Scatter in the fennel seeds and cook for 1 minute • Pour in the wine and bring to the boil • Tip the contents of the frying pan into the risotto pan • Pour in the rest of the stock • Give everything a good stir, put the lid back on and reduce the heat to medium • Cook for 8–9 minutes • Keep the frying pan for the next step

Meanwhile, roughly chop any chunky artichokes • Tip them, along with their oil, into the frying pan • Chop the hazelnuts and add them to the pan • Fry over a medium heat for about 3 minutes until the hazelnuts are golden and the artichokes are heated through • Zest one of the lemons over the top

Make a salad • Tip the rocket into a large salad bowl • Halve the zested lemon and squeeze the juice over the leaves • Add the remaining tablespoon of olive oil and a big pinch of salt and pepper and toss

Return to the risotto • Remove the lid and stir the risotto continuously for 1 minute, then halve the second lemon and squeeze over the juice • Grate in the plant-based parmesan, if using, and season to taste • If the rice is still firm, cook for a further 1 minute

Serve • Spoon the risotto into bowls and top with the artichoke and hazelnut mixture • Slice the chives and scatter them over the top

Crispy Mushroom Soup

This is a proper gourmet soup that you can get onto the table in under 30 minutes, using whatever mushrooms you've got in your fridge! The dried mushrooms are a great store-cupboard secret and add a punchy mushroom flavour to any dish. The peppery, earthy flavour of this soup is matched by its beautiful appearance, created by the drizzle of soy cream, our crispy fried mushrooms and the sage leaves.

Serves 4

500ml boiling water
1 vegetable stock pot or cube
20g dried mushrooms
    (we used porcini)
1 celery stick
1 carrot
½ onion
250g fresh mushrooms
    (any type)
1 tbsp olive oil
handful of sage leaves
150ml white wine
200ml plant-based cream

For the crispy fried mushrooms
230g shiitake mushrooms
1 tsp garlic powder
1 tsp smoked paprika
½ tsp ground white pepper
1 tsp dried oregano
1 tsp nutritional yeast
1 tbsp maple syrup
1 tbsp olive oil
salt and black pepper

To serve
4 tbsp plant-based cream
1 tbsp vegetable oil
4 sage leaves
sliced sourdough bread (optional)

Kettle boiled • Mixing jug • Food processor • Saucepan • Frying pan • Kitchen paper

Make the soup • Pour the boiling water into a jug • Add the stock pot or cube and the dried mushrooms, stir and set aside • Finely dice or use a food processor to chop the celery, carrot, onion and fresh mushrooms • Heat the olive oil in a saucepan over a medium heat • Add the chopped veg and the herbs • Fry for 5 minutes • Remove the rehydrated mushrooms from the stock, finely chop and add to the pan • Pour the mushroomy stock into the pan along with the white wine • Simmer for 5 minutes

Meanwhile, make the crispy fried mushrooms • Shred the shiitake mushrooms in a bowl • Add all the other 'chick'n' ingredients except the olive oil and mix until the mushrooms are well coated • Heat the olive oil in a frying pan over a medium heat • Add the mushroom mixture and fry for 10 minutes until caramelised and golden

Finish the soup • Pour the soup mixture into the food processor (you may need to do this in batches) • Add the 200ml plant-based cream and blitz until smooth • Pour the soup back into the pan and reheat

Serve • Spoon the soup into 4 bowls • Drizzle with the plant-based cream and top with a pile of the mushroom 'chick'n' • Wipe out the frying pan with kitchen paper and place it back over a medium heat • Add the vegetable oil and fry the sage leaves for about 2 minutes until crisp • Place a crispy leaf on top of each bowl • Serve the soup with slices of sourdough, if you like

Potato & Pickle Upside-Down Pie

The speedy trick to this flavour-packed pie is to have the pastry baking in the oven at the same time as you are making the filling. Once everything is cooked, you just need to put the two together and - hey presto - a pie! The lime pickle is a punchy taste but works wonders here. Used in moderation it gives a subtle undercurrent of spice to this delicious dish.

Serves 4

1 x 320g sheet of ready-rolled
    dairy-free puff pastry
400g potatoes
100g frozen peas
200g Tenderstem broccoli
1 tbsp light olive oil
150g lime pickle,
    or to taste
3 tbsp crispy onions
salt and black pepper

For the green sauce
25g frozen peas
small bunch of fresh coriander
50g baby spinach
1 tbsp light olive oil
salt and black pepper

Preheat oven to 200°C • Baking sheet • Saucepan • Kettle boiled • Large roasting tin • Food processor

Make the base • Unroll the pastry onto the baking sheet on its paper • Score a 2cm border all around the edges of the pastry with a sharp knife • Transfer to the hot oven and bake for 18 minutes

Make the filling • Peel the potatoes and cut them into 2cm cubes • Place in the saucepan, cover with boiling water and bring to the boil • Simmer for 7–10 minutes until cooked through • Add the peas for the last 2 minutes of cooking time • Drain and allow to steam dry for a few minutes, then tip back into the same pan

Pickle the greens • Toss the broccoli in the oil and the lime pickle • Spread out in the roasting tin and transfer to the oven • Cook for 10 minutes

Make the green sauce • Put the peas into a bowl and cover with boiling water • Reserving a few leaves for garnish, chop the coriander leaves and stalks • When the peas have defrosted, add them to the food processor with the chopped coriander • Add the spinach, oil and a pinch of salt and pepper • Blend to a paste – you may also need to add 1–2 tablespoons of water to loosen the mixture

Assemble • Add the green sauce to the pan with the potatoes and peas and mix well • Season to taste, then remove from the heat • Spoon over the pastry base, staying inside the border • Top with the broccoli and the pickle roasting juices • Scatter with the reserved coriander leaves and crispy onions

Black Bean Mole with Salsa

One of the most-loved dishes among the BOSH! food team, this dish comes highly recommended. This mole is rich, dark and smoky, and really tastes as though it's been bubbling away for hours to let the flavours develop and deepen. The salsa complements the mole with a lovely tangy freshness. It's a great option for a healthy yet comforting dinner, served with corn tortillas for scooping or with rice for a more substantial meal.

Serves 2

1 tbsp vegetable oil
1 onion
½ tsp lazy garlic or ½ garlic
    clove, crushed
1 tsp ground cinnamon
1 tsp ground coriander
1 tsp ground cumin
1 tsp smoked paprika
1 x 400g tin black beans
100ml water
½ x 100g tin chipotles in adobo
    or 1 tsp dried chipotle flakes
    and 1 tbsp tomato purée
30g dark chocolate
½ orange
smoked salt

For the salsa
100g cherry tomatoes
2 spring onions
½ fresh red chilli
dash of red wine vinegar
½ lime
large handful of fresh coriander,
    leaves and stems
salt

To serve
pumpkin and/or sunflower seeds
corn tortillas or cooked rice
    (optional)

Heavy-based saucepan on a medium heat • Frying pan

Start the mole • Add the oil to the hot saucepan • Roughly dice the onion and add it to the pan along with the garlic and spices • Fry for 10 minutes, stirring from time to time • Drain the black beans and add them to the pan along with the fresh water • Add the chipotles or chilli flakes and the tomato purée • Increase the heat to medium-high • Let it bubble for 3–5 minutes, until thickened

Toast the seeds • Put the frying pan on a medium-high heat • Once the pan is hot, scatter over a handful of pumpkin and/or sunflower seeds • Toast until browned and the seeds smell good • Take off the heat and set aside

Make the salsa • Roughly chop the cherry tomatoes, spring onions and red chilli and put them in a bowl • Add the red wine vinegar and salt, and squeeze in the juice of the lime • Saving a handful of leaves for garnish, roughly chop the coriander leaves and stems and add them to the bowl • Stir to combine

Finish the mole • Roughly chop the dark chocolate • Add it to the pan and stir until melted • Squeeze in the juice of the orange • Season with smoked salt and stir through

Serve • Spoon the mole into deep bowls • Top with the salsa, toasted seeds and coriander leaves • Serve with tortillas or rice on the side

Red Wine Cassoulet

We've sped up the classic cassoulet without sacrificing any of the flavour by removing all the stewing time. Rich red wine, stock and prunes bring depth to this speedy stew. Serve with chopped fresh herbs and a generous spoonful of mustard. For the best results, use the most flavourful sausages you can find and a lovely, rich red wine as the base for the sauce – you only need a glass or so, so the rest goes to the cook!

Serves 4

3 small leeks
2 tbsp, plus 1 tsp light olive oil
100g soft prunes
300ml red wine
500ml vegetable stock
5 thyme sprigs
2–3 tsp yeast extract
1 heaped tbsp tomato purée
350g potatoes
4 garlic cloves
4–8 plant-based sausages
50g chopped walnuts
1 x 400g tin cannellini
    or haricot beans
handful of fresh flat-leaf
    parsley (optional)
salt and black pepper

To serve

1 x 60g packet rocket salad
Dijon or wholegrain mustard

Preheat oven to 200°C • Wide shallow casserole with a lid on a medium heat • Medium saucepan • Mandolin or box grater with a slicing blade • Roasting pan • Line 2 baking trays

Cook the leeks • Cut the leeks into 2cm slices • Add 2 tablespoons of the oil to the hot casserole • Once it's gently sizzling, add the leeks • Cook for 6–8 minutes, stirring occasionally, until lightly golden and softened

Meanwhile, make the sauce • Remove and discard the stones from the prunes and roughly chop • Add to the hot saucepan along with the wine, 150ml of the stock, the thyme sprigs, the yeast extract and the tomato purée • Bring to the boil • Let bubble for 10 minutes

Add the potatoes and garlic • Meanwhile, peel and thinly slice the potatoes • Peel and crush the garlic • Reduce the heat under the leeks to low • Add the garlic and potato slices to the casserole and stir for 1 minute

Cook the sausages and toast the walnuts • Toss the sausages in the remaining oil and lay them out on a baking tray • Transfer to the hot oven and bake according to the packet instructions (about 10–12 minutes) • Spread the walnuts over the second tray • Bake for 5 minutes, then remove and set aside to cool

Finish the casserole • Season the leek and potato mixture with salt and pepper • Pour in the sauce along with the rest of the stock • Bring to the boil, cover with the lid and simmer fast for 10 minutes, or until the potatoes are tender • Drain the beans, then add them to the pot along with the toasted walnuts for the last few minutes of cooking time to heat through • Chop the parsley, if using, and stir it through • Serve with the rocket salad and mustard alongside

Salsa Gnocchi

Gnocchi are delicious little Italian dumplings, which are now very easy to find in most supermarkets. Gnocchi are a little misunderstood and often overlooked – which is a shame because, like pasta, rice and couscous, they can form the bulk of a satisfying meal. With this recipe we've married Italian gnocchi with Mexican salsa. If you've never tried gnocchi before, pick up a pack next time you're at the shops and give this recipe a go – we're pretty sure you'll love it!

Serves 2

1 x 500g packet gnocchi
4 large fresh tomatoes
1 shallot or small onion
1 garlic clove
½ fresh red chilli
1 tbsp red wine vinegar
3 tbsp olive oil, plus extra for drizzling
small handful of fresh basil leaves
1 tbsp grated plant-based
    parmesan (optional)
salt and black pepper

Large saucepan of salted water on a high heat • Small food processor • Large frying pan

Cook the gnocchi • Drop the gnocchi into the pan of boiling water • Cook according to the instructions on the packet, then drain

Meanwhile, make the salsa sauce • Halve the tomatoes and use a teaspoon to scoop out and discard the watery seeds • Chop one of the tomatoes into small dice and set it aside for later • Trim the onion, garlic and chilli • Add the remaining tomato halves, onion, garlic, red wine vinegar, chilli and 1 tablespoon of the olive oil to the food processor • Pulse until you have a chunky salsa (or use a knife to finely chop, if you prefer) • Season with salt and pepper

Fry the gnocchi • Put the frying pan on a high heat • Add the remaining 2 tablespoons of olive oil • Tip the gnocchi into the hot oil and fry for 5–6 minutes, until golden and crisping around the edges

Add the salsa • Tip the salsa into the frying pan and toss it through the gnocchi • Once hot, remove from the heat and stir in the fresh chopped tomato • Stir through most of the basil, reserving a few leaves for garnish

Serve • Drizzle the gnocchi with a little olive oil and top with the reserved basil leaves • Sprinkle with grated plant-based parmesan, if you like

Super Meaty Spag Bol

Spaghetti Bolognese is a family favourite in the BOSH! household. We all live together and we like to cook it for each other at least once a week, so we had to make a speedy version. For this recipe we blitz up some high-quality plant-based sausages, then brown them. Spring onions are quick to sauté, so we can make our bolognese sauce in the same time the pasta takes to cook. Absolutely ingenious, and a great way to satisfy the whole family after a long day! This dish was inspired by Ian's family tradition of eating spag bol on a Monday night, but you can eat it any night of the week.

Serves 4

1 celery stick
1 small carrot
4 plant-based sausages
handful of thyme and/or sage leaves
1 tbsp tomato purée
½ tsp lazy garlic or ½ garlic
   clove, crushed
1 tsp fennel seeds
2 tbsp olive oil
2 tbsp balsamic vinegar
1 tsp soy sauce
1 tsp nutritional yeast
1 x 400g tin chopped tomatoes
1 tbsp ketchup
1 bay leaf
1 cinnamon stick
½ orange

For the spaghetti
2 tbsp fine sea salt
400g spaghetti

To serve
plant-based parmesan
extra-virgin olive oil

Large saucepan half-full of water on a high heat • Kettle boiled • Food processor • Large frying pan on a medium heat • Tongs

Blitz the bolognese mixture • Roughly chop the celery stick • Peel and roughly chop the carrot • Add both to the food processor along with the sausages and pulse until finely chopped • Add the thyme or sage leaves, tomato purée, garlic and fennel seeds and pulse a few more times

Cook the bolognese • Heat the olive oil in the frying pan • Tip in the mince mixture and stir fry for a few minutes • Add the balsamic vinegar, soy sauce, nutritional yeast, chopped tomatoes, ketchup, bay leaf and cinnamon stick • Squeeze in the juice from the orange • Stir and leave to simmer while you cook the pasta

Cook the pasta • Top up the water in the pasta pan with water from the kettle • Add the salt and bring back to the boil • Add the spaghetti and cook until al dente, following the instructions on the packet

To finish • Remove the cinnamon stick and bay leaf from the bolognese and discard • Use tongs to slosh the cooked pasta into the frying pan with the sauce, bringing some of the pasta water with it as you do so • Mix everything together with the tongs, adding more pasta water to loosen, if needed • Serve with plant-based parmesan and a drizzle of good olive oil

Theasby's Tempeh Toastie

Toastie? Completed it mate. We challenge anyone in the land to make a tastier toastie in under 30 minutes. Expect balsamic wonderfulness on your tongue from our quick caramelised onions, meaty umami from our tempeh bacon, smoky gooey delight from the high-quality smoked cheese, all toasted to perfection inside thick-cut sourdough. Cheesus! The Earl of Sandwich would be proud.

Serves 2

1 tbsp olive oil
4 thick slices sourdough bread

For the caramelised onions
1 red onion
1 tbsp plant-based butter
1 tbsp balsamic vinegar
1 tbsp soft brown sugar
½ tsp salt

For the tempeh bacon
1 tbsp plant-based butter
1 tsp fennel seeds
100g tempeh
1 tsp smoked paprika
1 tbsp maple syrup
½ tsp soy sauce or tamari

For the smoked cheese mix
handful of chives
1 tbsp dairy-free cream cheese
60g smoked dairy-free cheese
1 tbsp Dijon mustard
1 tsp oat milk
½ tsp sherry or red wine vinegar
black pepper

Small saucepan with a lid on a medium heat • Frying pan • Line a tray with kitchen paper • Sandwich iron or heavy pan that will fit inside the frying pan

Start with the caramelised onions • Peel and thinly slice the onion • Melt the plant-based butter in the small saucepan • Add the onion to the pan along with the balsamic vinegar, sugar and salt • Stir, reduce the heat to the lowest setting and put the lid on the pan

Make the tempeh bacon • Put the frying pan on a medium heat and melt the plant-based butter • Crush the fennel seeds and cut the tempeh into thin slices • Add both to the pan along with the smoked paprika • Carefully turn the tempeh slices in the spiced butter to coat, then pour over the maple syrup and soy sauce or tamari • Fry the tempeh in the sticky mixture for about 10 minutes until starting to crisp and caramelise • Remove the tempeh to the tray lined with kitchen paper and set aside • Rinse and dry the pan

Meanwhile, make the smoked cheese mix • Chop the chives and put them in a bowl with the rest of the cheese mix ingredients • Mix everything together with a fork

Finish the sandwich • Put the frying pan back over a medium heat and add the tablespoon of olive oil, ensuring it coats the base of the pan evenly • Lay 2 slices of bread in the pan • Top each slice first with the cheese mix, then the tempeh bacon • Divide the onions between the slices • Lay the remaining bread slices on top • Use your biggest, heaviest pan or a sandwich iron to compress the sandwiches • Fry for 3–4 minutes, then remove the weight, very carefully flip the sandwiches over and replace the weight on top • Fry for another 3–4 minutes • Remove the sandwiches to a wooden board, cut in half and serve

Ultimate Vegan Mac & Cheese

There's something about creamy, cheesy pasta that just works. Mac & Cheese is perhaps the perfect example of this, and that's why it's become a vegan street food classic all over the world. This speedy version is exceptionally creamy, incredibly cheesy and wonderfully crunchy. Coupled with a fresh salad it's the stuff of dreams. Choose a vegan cheese you like the taste of and stick with it, then you know it'll taste good.

Serves 4–6

300g macaroni
750ml unsweetened plant-based milk
50g cashew nuts
40ml olive oil
1 garlic clove
40g flour
100g dairy-free cheese
3 tbsp nutritional yeast
2 tsp Dijon mustard
50g fresh breadcrumbs
2 tbsp olive oil
salt and black pepper

Preheat grill to high • Large saucepan of salted water on a high heat • Medium saucepan on a medium-high heat • Nutribullet or other power blender • Large ovenproof frying pan • Microplane or fine grater • Whisk

Cook the mac • Bring the pan of salted water to the boil • Add the macaroni and cook for 1 minute less than stated on the packet instructions • Drain

Meanwhile, make the nut milk mixture • Put the almond milk and cashews into the medium saucepan and bring to the boil • Transfer the mixture to the power blender and blitz until smooth

Make the sauce • Put the frying pan over a medium heat and add the olive oil • Peel the garlic and grate it straight into the pan • Cook for a couple of minutes until just starting to brown • Add the flour to the pan and whisk until it combines with the garlicky oil to make a paste • Cook for 1 minute • Reduce the heat to low • Slowly pour in a little of the nut milk mixture and whisk until completely combined • Keep adding more, little by little, whisking until all the nut milk is incorporated • Cook for 2 minutes • Grate the dairy-free cheese • Add the nutritional yeast, mustard and cheese to the pan • Stir to mix, adding a splash more almond milk if the mixture is too thick • Taste and season generously with salt and pepper • Drain the cooked macaroni • Take the pan of sauce off the heat and tip in the drained pasta • Stir to coat the pasta in the sauce

Make the topping • Put the breadcrumbs, olive oil and a big pinch of salt and pepper into a bowl and stir to mix • Scatter the crumbs over the pasta

Finish • Place the pan under the grill and cook for 2–3 minutes, keeping a close eye on it, until the topping is crispy • Serve

Goulash & Dumplings

This dish is a perfect winter warmer – deep, rich, hot and bursting with umami tomato and paprika flavours. Goulash can be made just as well by subbing out the meat and letting the veggies sing and we've also included some super-fast dumplings to cook in the pan and soak up all the wonderful flavours.

Serves 4

2 tbsp light olive oil
1 large onion
1 large carrot
2 red peppers
4 garlic cloves
1 tsp caraway seeds
1 x 400g tin finely chopped tomatoes
500ml water or veg stock
2 bay leaves
1 fresh red chilli
1 tsp caster sugar
1 tbsp sweet smoked paprika
2 x 400g tins cannellini or
    borlotti beans
salt and black pepper

For the dumplings
handful of flat-leaf parsley
150g plain flour
½ tsp salt
1 tsp baking powder
50ml light olive oil, plus
    extra to oil hands
75ml unsweetened plant-based milk
1–2 tsp Dijon mustard

To serve
handful of flat-leaf parsley
1 lemon
plant-based yoghurt or plant-based
    sour cream
salad of your choice

Wide, shallow casserole with a lid on a medium heat • Medium saucepan on a medium heat

Start the goulash • Add the oil to the casserole • Peel and finely slice the onion • Peel the carrot and slice into 5mm rounds • Add both to the casserole and fry for 10 minutes, stirring occasionally • Roughly chop the peppers and add them to the pan • Crush the garlic and add it to the casserole along with the caraway seeds • Stir-fry for 1 minute

Meanwhile, make the tomato sauce • Put the tinned tomatoes into the medium saucepan • Once simmering, add the water or stock and stir to combine • Break the bay leaves and add them to the pan • Deseed and roughly chop the chilli and add it to the pan along with the sugar and paprika • Bring to the boil • Reduce the heat and simmer for 10 minutes

Meanwhile, make the dumplings • Chop the parsley and put it into a bowl • Add the flour, salt and baking powder and mix well • Make a well in the mixture, pour in the oil, plant-based milk and mustard • Mix until it comes together • Grease your hands and roll the dough into 16 equal-sized balls

Finish the goulash • Drain the tinned beans through a sieve and tip into the casserole along with the tomato sauce • Mix well and bring to the boil • Add the dumplings, cover and reduce the heat • Simmer for 8 minutes • Season to taste

Serve • Chop the parsley and sprinkle it over the goulash • Chop the lemon into wedges • Serve with the yoghurt or sour cream, salad and the lemon wedges for squeezing over the top

Simple One-Pot Spaghetti

Perfect for those nights when you're hungry but can't be bothered to cook, this dish is truly effortless to throw together – simply let the pan do the work. The creamy sauce is made from the spaghetti cooking in its own water. We know it's not traditional, but it works! And what's more, it's quick, satisfying and downright delicious. Another bonus is that you make it all in one pot, which means there's hardly any washing up. Yay!

Serves 4–6

2 tbsp olive oil, plus extra
  for drizzling
1 onion
2 garlic cloves
1 tsp chilli flakes
500g cherry tomatoes
1 litre boiling water
1 vegetable stock cube
500g spaghetti
4 tbsp pine nuts
small bunch of fresh basil leaves
1 lemon
200g spinach
3 tbsp capers
salt and black pepper

Kettle boiled • Large saucepan or casserole with a lid on a medium heat • Microplane or fine grater • Frying pan

Build up the pot • Pour the olive oil into the hot pan • Peel and slice the onion and add it to the hot oil • Fry for 2 minutes, stirring occasionally • Peel the garlic and grate it directly into the pan • Add the chilli flakes • Tip in the cherry tomatoes • Pour in the boiling water and add the stock cube • Increase the heat to high and bring to the boil • Add the pasta • Cover the pan and reduce the heat to medium-high • Cook for 10 minutes until the pasta has absorbed the liquid, stirring occasionally to prevent it sticking

Toast the pine nuts • Put a frying pan over a medium heat • Sprinkle over the pine nuts and toast until golden • Take off the heat

Add the lemon and herbs • Reserve a few basil leaves for garnish and roughly chop the rest • Slice the lemon in half • Remove the pan lid and stir in the spinach along with the capers and the chopped basil – it looks like a lot but it will quickly wilt down • Squeeze in the lemon juice • Taste and season with salt and black pepper

Serve • Divide the pasta between 4 bowls • Top each portion with a drizzle of olive oil, 1 tablespoon of the toasted pine nuts, the reserved basil leaves and a good crack of black pepper

Takeaways

02

Speedy Restaurant Ramen

We've made this ramen recipe – inspired by a trip to Los Angeles – countless times. You can play around with the ingredients here – if you can't find the gyoza, then plant-based chicken is a great alternative, and you can use other greens instead of the beans, if you like. Try to find the liquid miso soup sachets (rather than powder) for the best, most delicious broth. Also, if you can't find king oyster mushrooms, a handful of any type will do.

Serves 2

500ml boiling water
2 vegan miso soup sachets
1 red onion
1 king oyster mushroom
2 tbsp vegetable oil
1 tbsp nutritional yeast
½ tsp lazy garlic or ½ garlic
    clove, crushed
thumb-sized piece of fresh ginger
100g green beans
200g straight-to-wok udon noodles
100g frozen edamame beans

For the crispy miso aubergine
1 aubergine
1 tsp vegetable oil
1 tsp miso paste
1 tsp soy sauce
1 tsp rice vinegar

For the gyoza
1 tbsp vegetable oil
4 frozen vegan gyoza dumplings
2 tbsp water

To serve
2 spring onions
handful of fresh coriander
sesame seeds
chilli oil
soy sauce
pickled ginger

Preheat grill to high • Kettle boiled • Line a baking tray • Heatproof jug • Medium saucepan • Microplane or fine grater • Steamer pan or colander • Frying pan with a lid

Start with the aubergine • Trim the aubergine and slice it into half-moons • Grease the lined tray with oil • Put the miso paste, soy sauce and rice vinegar into a small bowl and mix to combine • Brush half the marinade all over the aubergine slices and lay them on the baking tray • Grill for 1–2 minutes on each side until golden brown and crisp at the edges • Set aside

Make the ramen broth • Pour the boiling water into a heatproof jug • Add the miso soup and mix well • Peel and quarter the onion • Shred the mushroom • Heat the oil in a saucepan over a medium heat • Add the onion and mushroom along with the remaining marinade and the nutritional yeast • Add the garlic and grate the ginger directly into the pan • Stir-fry for about 5 minutes until the onion and mushrooms are starting to caramelise • Pour in the miso soup and bring to a simmer

Steam the noodles • Trim the green beans • Place a steamer pan or colander above the ramen broth and add the noodles, edamame beans and green beans • Cover and steam for 3–5 minutes to warm through

Meanwhile, cook the gyoza • Heat the oil in a frying pan over a medium-high heat • Add the gyoza and fry for 1 minute • Add the water, cover the pan and steam for 3–4 minutes

Serve • Divide the noodles, edamame and green beans between two deep bowls • Remove the onion from the broth and discard • Ladle the broth over the noodles • Top with the grilled aubergine slices and gyoza • Finely slice the spring onions and coriander and sprinkle them over the top along with some sesame seeds • Season with chilli oil, soy sauce and pickled ginger

Got-No-Beef Rendang

Rendang, typically made with super-tender meat and an incredibly thick spiced coconut gravy, is one of Asia's most popular dishes. All our food is meat-free, but that doesn't mean we don't rendang! In this super-speedy version we use the wonderful texture of jackfruit as our hero ingredient, all snuggled up in a thick, deliciously spicy blanket. Incredible. And super speedy.

Serves 4

2 x 400g tin jackfruit
2 tsp steak seasoning
2 tbsp vegetable oil
1 x 400ml tin coconut milk
4 tbsp desiccated coconut
1 tbsp tamarind paste or lime juice
1 fresh green chilli
small bunch of fresh coriander

For the spice paste

1 lemongrass stalk
1 onion
3 garlic cloves
thumb-sized piece fresh ginger
1 tsp dried chilli flakes
1 tsp ground cinnamon
1 tsp ground turmeric
1 tsp sugar

To serve

2 x 250g pouches basmati rice
600ml water
large pinch of salt
4 dairy-free naan or chapati

Preheat oven to 220°C • Line a baking tray • Microwaveable bowl • Microwave • Food processor • 2 large frying pans • Clean tea towel

Roast the jackfruit • Drain the jackfruit and chop it into bite-sized chunks • Tip onto the lined baking tray and gently squash the pieces down with a fork • Sprinkle over the steak seasoning and drizzle with 1 tablespoon of the vegetable oil • Toss well • Put the tray in the oven to roast for 10–15 minutes

Cook the rice • Tip the rice into a microwaveable bowl • Add the water and a large pinch of salt • Microwave on high for 10 minutes

Make the spice paste • Roughly chop the lemongrass • Halve and peel the onion • Peel the garlic and ginger • Add everything to a food processor and blitz to a paste

Make the curry • Put a large frying pan over a medium-high heat • Add the remaining 1 tablespoon of oil • Add the spice paste to the hot oil and fry for about 4 minutes until it begins to brown – it should smell really fragrant • Tip in the coconut milk and stir to combine • Leave to bubble away

Prepare the bread • Remove the rice from the microwave • Cover with a tea towel and set aside • Put the naan or chapatis in the microwave and cook on high for 1 minute

Return to the curry • Remove the jackfruit from the oven and tip it into the curry • Cook for another 3 minutes • Heat the other frying pan over a medium heat • Add the desiccated coconut and dry fry, shaking constantly, until golden • Tip the majority of the toasted coconut into the curry, stir, then remove from the heat • Season the curry with the tamarind paste or lime juice

Finish and serve • Heat the rice pouches in the microwave according to the packet instructions • Finely slice the green chilli and chop the coriander • Sprinkle over the curry along with the remaining toasted coconut • Serve with the rice and naan or chapatis

Jackfruit Rendang Burger

We love rendang so much that we had to stick it in the book twice! Less traditional than the curry in the previous recipe, here it is served in buns and topped with a deliciously fresh mix of lime, red onion, chilli and cucumber and garnished with fragrant toasted coconut. This was inspired by a trip Henry and his fiancée Em-J took to Bali in a past life, where the food was incredible. A great, flavour-packed dish to serve for Friday-night beers with friends (or on a beach overlooking a beautiful Indonesian sunset!).

Serves 4

2 x 400g tins jackfruit
2 tsp steak seasoning
2 tbsp vegetable oil
200ml coconut milk
4 tbsp desiccated coconut
salt and black pepper

For the spice paste
1 lemongrass stalk
1 onion
3 garlic cloves
thumb-sized piece fresh ginger
1 tsp dried chilli flakes
1 tsp ground turmeric
1 tsp ground cinnamon
1 tsp sugar

For the red onion topping
1 lime
1 red onion
½ cucumber
1 fresh green chilli

To serve
4 burger buns
a small bunch of coriander leaves

Preheat oven to 220°C • Line a baking tray • Food processor • 2 large frying pans

Roast the jackfruit • Drain the jackfruit and chop it into bite-sized chunks • Tip onto the lined baking tray and gently squash the pieces down with a fork • Sprinkle over the steak seasoning and drizzle with 1 tablespoon of the vegetable oil • Toss well • Put the tray in the oven to roast for 10–15 minutes

Make the spice paste • Chop the lemongrass • Halve and peel the onion • Peel the garlic and ginger • Put all the ingredients in a food processor and blitz to a paste

Make the curry • Put a large frying pan over a medium-high heat • Heat the other tablespoon of oil • Add the spice paste and fry for 4–5 minutes until it begins to brown and smell really fragrant • Tip in the coconut milk and stir to combine • Leave to bubble away

Make the topping • Halve the lime • Peel the red onion and trim the chilli • Finely slice the onion, chilli and cucumber • Place in a bowl • Squeeze in the juice of one lime half • Season well and toss to combine

Return to the curry • Remove the jackfruit from the oven and tip it into the curry • Cook for a further 3 minutes • Heat the other frying pan over a medium heat • Scatter over the desiccated coconut and dry-fry, shaking constantly, until golden • Tip the majority of the toasted coconut into the curry • Squeeze in the juice from the remaining lime half and season well

Assemble the burgers • Halve the burger buns • Pick the coriander leaves • Divide the jackfruit rendang between the burger bases • Top with the red onion topping, some coriander leaves and the remaining desiccated coconut • Sandwich with the burger tops and tuck in!

Beetroot & Lentil Burger

These showstopping burgers are piled high and sandwiched with crispy salad, tomatoes, gherkins, cheese and a generous helping of our favourite burger sauce. It's worth looking out for super-soft vegan brioche buns for these as they really tip them over the edge into something that is very special indeed. When shaping your burgers, don't worry about making them perfectly round – the rough edges make for nice crispy bits!

Makes 2 double-decker burgers or 4 single-deckers if you increase the bun quantities

120g cooked beetroot
80g rolled oats
30g plain or gram flour
60g pre-cooked lentils
1 tsp smoked paprika
1 tsp garam masala
1 tsp ground turmeric
½ tsp curry powder
½ green chilli
pinch of salt
2 tbsp vegetable oil
a few gratings of fresh ginger

For the wedges
1 large or 2 small sweet potatoes
2 tbsp olive oil
1 tbsp coriander seeds
1 small fresh red chilli
salt

Preheat oven to 250°C • Line 2 baking trays • Microplane or fine grater • Cut out 4 x 12cm squares of parchment paper • Pestle and mortar • Food processor • Steamer or saucepan with a colander • Kettle boiled • Frying pan with a lid

Start with the wedges • Cut the sweet potatoes into 1cm wedges and lay them on a lined baking tray • Pour over the olive oil and a few generous pinches of salt • Put the tray on the top shelf of the oven to bake for 15 minutes, until cooked through and golden brown

Meanwhile, make the burgers • Put all the ingredients, except the oil, in a food processor and blitz to a paste • Spoon the mixture equally into the centre of the prepared parchment squares and use wet hands to flatten the mixture into thin patties • Fill the base of the steamer pan or saucepan with boiling water and set over a medium heat • Place the parchment squares in the steamer pan or colander and set over the boiling water • Cover and steam the burgers for 3 minutes, then remove

Cook the burgers • Set a frying pan over a medium heat • Add the vegetable oil • Carefully slide the patties into the hot oil and fry for about 5 minutes on each side, until browned and cooked through, flipping once

Return to the wedges • Bash the coriander seeds in a pestle and mortar • Deseed and finely chop the chilli • Scatter the coriander seeds and chilli over the wedges and return to the oven for another 5 minutes

Prepare the burger buns • Take one of the buns and slice off the top and bottom to create a middle bun for your burger, Big Mac style! • Put the buns on a baking tray and place in the oven below the sweet potato wedges for 5 minutes to warm through • Give the wedges a shake

For the burger sauce
½ large gherkin, plus a dash
of brine from the jar
2 tbsp egg-free mayo
1 tbsp ketchup
1 tsp Tabasco

To serve
3 burger buns
4 slices dairy-free cheese
2 crisp lettuce leaves
1 large tomato
½ large gherkin

Make the burger sauce ⸱ Finely chop the half gherkin and put it in a bowl with the brine ⸱ Add the mayo, ketchup and Tabasco and mix to combine ⸱ Set aside

Finish the burgers ⸱ Check your burgers are nicely sealed on both sides, then lay the cheese slices on top of each burger ⸱ Turn the heat right down, add a splash of water and cover the pan with the lid ⸱ Get your buns from the oven and start building!

Build the burgers ⸱ Start with a spoonful of burger sauce on each bottom and middle bun ⸱ Slice the remaining half gherkin and pile the slices onto each bottom bun, topping them with a slice of lettuce ⸱ Slide a cheese-topped patty on top ⸱ Cover with the middle bun, followed by 2 tomato slices and the second cheese-topped patty from the pan ⸱ Add the top bun and gently press down

Serve ⸱ Remove the wedges and serve up with your burgers, along with any leftover burger sauce for dipping and loads of napkins, because it will get juicy!

Butter Tofu Curry

This dish was inspired by one of the world's most popular Indian dishes, butter chicken. We just replaced the chicken with wonderful puff tofu and made the recipe speedy! Ordering curry from the local curry house is always a bit of a gamble. Sometimes it's great but sometimes it's just 'meh'. Next time you're in the mood for a rich, creamy curry that's full of flavour and completely reliable, give this recipe a whirl. Goes great with chapatis or a quick side salad.

Serves 4

2 tbsp plant-based butter
1 onion
2 tsp garam masala
2 tsp ground coriander
2 tsp ground cumin
2 tsp ground turmeric
1 garlic clove
thumb-sized piece fresh ginger
1 tbsp tomato purée
400ml passata
200ml coconut or oat cream
salt and black pepper

For the tofu puffs
2 x 225g blocks firm
    (or pressed) tofu
4 tbsp cornflour
large pinch of salt
vegetable oil, for frying

To serve
2 x 250g pouches basmati rice
2 limes
1 fresh green chilli
handful of fresh coriander leaves
plant-based naans or roti (optional)

2 large frying pans or casserole dishes • Microplane or fine grater • Kitchen paper • Sandwich bag or Tupperware container • Line a plate with kitchen paper

Start with the curry • Add 1 tablespoon of the plant-based butter to a frying pan or casserole and set over a medium-high heat • Peel and roughly chop the onion and add it to the pan with pinch of salt • Fry for 3–4 minutes, stirring occasionally • Add the spices and cook for 1 minute • Peel the garlic • Grate the garlic and ginger directly into the pan • Add the tomato purée and fry for 2 minutes • Pour the passata into the pan, bring to the boil, then reduce to a simmer • Leave to bubble while you make the puffs

Prepare the tofu puffs • Pour a 1cm depth of oil into the second frying pan and set it over a high heat • Pat the tofu dry with kitchen paper and tear it into bite-sized chunks • Put the cornflour and salt into a sandwich bag or Tupperware container • Add the tofu chunks and shake until the chunks are well dusted • Carefully lower the dusted tofu pieces into the hot oil and cook until golden, crispy and puffed up, increasing the heat if necessary • Remove to drain on the plate lined with kitchen paper

Prepare the accompaniments • Heat the rice pouches in the microwave according to the packet instructions • Slice the limes into wedges • Finely slice the green chilli

Return to the curry • Add the plant-based cream and the remaining tablespoon of plant-based butter to the pan • Season with salt and pepper • Tip the puffed tofu into the curry sauce and stir until coated

Serve • Divide the curry between bowls • Scatter with coriander leaves and green chilli • Serve with the rice, lime wedges and naans or roti, if you like

Jackfruit Shawarma

When we were younger, we weren't afraid of a questionable kebab after a night out. However, with age comes wisdom... But, rather than banish kebabs to the annals of time, we decided to make some that challenge the stereotype. These beauties are bursting with flavour and texture, and they're really healthy. The sumac in the pickled onions is optional, but it is easier to find now and adds a great citrus tang and pop of colour.

Serves 4

1 x 400g tin jackfruit
1 lemon
1 tsp ground allspice
1 tsp ground cinnamon
1 tsp ground cumin
½ tsp ground turmeric
½ tsp smoked paprika
1 tbsp pomegranate molasses
2 tbsp vegetable oil
1 onion
½ tsp lazy garlic or ½ garlic
    clove, crushed
½ tsp cumin seeds
1 tbsp nutritional yeast

For the garlic tahini dressing
2 tbsp tahini
1 tbsp plant-based yoghurt
½ tsp lazy garlic or ½ garlic
    clove, crushed
salt and black pepper

For the quick pickled onions
½ red onion
2 tbsp red wine vinegar
1 tsp salt
1 tsp sugar
½ tsp sumac (optional)

To serve
1 baby gem lettuce
2 large tomatoes
½ cucumber
4 pitta breads
4 jarred pickled chillies
chilli sauce of your choice
    or harissa

Preheat grill to high or have the toaster ready • Frying pan over a medium heat

Make the shawarma • Rinse and drain the jackfruit and put it in a bowl • Halve the lemon and squeeze the juice of half over the jackfruit, reserving the other half • Add the spices and pomegranate molasses and stir to thoroughly coat the jackfruit • Add the oil to the hot pan • Peel and finely slice the onion and add to the pan with the garlic • Add the jackfruit, cumin seeds and nutritional yeast and fry for 8–10 minutes, breaking the jackfruit up a little as you stir

Make the garlic tahini dressing • Place all the sauce ingredients in a bowl with a splash of water • Squeeze over the juice from the reserved lemon half • Whisk together, adding enough water to loosen until the dressing has a pouring consistency • Season to taste

Make the quick pickled onions • Peel and thinly slice the red onion and add to a bowl • Add the other ingredients and mix well, stirring to help the sugar and salt dissolve • Squeeze the onions in your hands to help break them down and pickle quickly

To serve • Roughly slice the lettuce, tomatoes and cucumber • Toast the pittas • Using a sharp knife, open one side of each pitta to create a pocket • Divide the lettuce, tomatoes and cucumber between the pittas • Spoon in portions of the shawarma mixture • Drizzle over the dressing and finish each kebab with the pickled onions, pickled chillies and some chilli sauce or harissa, as you wish

Luxurious Rice Pilaf

This special little rice number is full of colour, bejewelled with sweetness and bursting with crunch. What's more, it's made with a whole load of storecupboard ingredients, so it's easy to make when you've not got much in. It's basically just an assembly job and we use pre-cooked rice to make it even faster. BOSH!

Serves 2–4 as a main

2 tbsp coconut oil
1 x 250g pouch pre-cooked basmati rice
1 tsp ground cumin
1 tsp garam masala
1 cinnamon stick
2 cardamom pods
100ml vegan stock
1 tbsp desiccated coconut
40g golden sultanas
salt and black pepper

For the crispy shallots
2 banana shallots
1 tbsp vegetable oil

For the toppings
40g flaked almonds
40g pistachios
½ red chilli
1 orange (optional)
handful of dried rose petals (optional)

For the quick kofte
2 tbsp vegetable oil
4 plant-based sausages
1 tsp cumin seeds
1 tsp ground cinnamon
1 tsp ground coriander

To serve
flatbreads
coconut yoghurt
fresh coriander leaves

Defrost the sausages, if frozen • 2 large frying pans over medium heat • Line a plate with kitchen paper • Clean tea towel

Make the crispy shallots • Peel and finely slice the shallots • Heat the vegetable oil in one of the frying pans • Add the shallots and fry for about 10 minutes, stirring occasionally, until dark brown and starting to crisp • Remove to drain on kitchen paper

Meanwhile, make the pilaf • Completely melt the coconut oil in the second frying pan • Add the rice, ground cumin, garam masala and the cinnamon stick and stir to coat the rice • Crush the cardamom pods with the flat of a knife, remove the seeds and add the seeds to the pan • Add the stock and desiccated coconut and stir gently so as not to break up the grains • Turn off the heat, season with salt and pepper and stir • Sprinkle over the sultanas • Cover the pan with a tea towel and set aside

Prepare the toppings • Wipe the shallot pan clean and put it back on the heat • Add flaked almonds and toast for 3–4 minutes, until golden, shaking the pan and watching carefully to ensure they don't burn • Remove and set aside • Lightly crush the pistachios • Trim and finely dice the chilli

Make the quick kofte • Wipe the pan clean again and add the vegetable oil • Chop the sausages into chunks and add them to the pan (or snip them in using kitchen scissors) • Add the spices and stir to coat the sausages • Fry for 3–4 minutes, until caramelised

Serve • Tip the rice onto a platter and top with the quick kofte, toasted almonds, crushed pistachios and crispy shallots • Sprinkle over the chilli and zest the orange, if using, directly over the top • Scatter over the rose petals, if using • Serve with flatbreads, coconut yoghurt and a sprinkling of fresh coriander leaves

Quick Tandoori Kebabs

Henry's mum showed him how to make a tandoori mix many years ago, way before he went plant-based. It's all about good-quality yoghurt and wonderful spices (and if you want a shortcut you can even buy ready-made tandoori spice). For this recipe, we're using our own spice mix alongside plant-based chick'n' chunks to create a wonderful kebab-shop-style kebab with a delicious mint raita. Get your grill hot hot HOT, to mirror the tandoor oven, and get ready for a marinaded masterpiece of a fakeaway!

Serves 4

500g plant-based chick'n chunks
2 limes

For the marinade
1 garlic clove
thumb-sized piece of fresh ginger
200g coconut yoghurt
1 tbsp tomato purée
1 tbsp garam masala
2 tsp hot smoked paprika
1 tsp ground cumin
1 tsp ground turmeric
1 tsp salt

For the raita
½ cucumber
handful of fresh mint leaves
150g coconut yoghurt
salt and black pepper

To serve
4 dairy-free naans, chapatis or rotis
3 spring onions
handful of fresh coriander
1 tsp chilli flakes (optional)

Preheat grill to high • Microplane or fine grater • Line a baking tray with wet baking paper

Make the marinade • Peel and grate the garlic and ginger into a bowl • Add the remaining ingredients for the marinade and mix well

Marinate the chick'n • Add the chick'n chunks to the marinade and toss to coat • Tip the contents of the bowl onto the lined baking tray • Slice the limes in half and put them on the side of the tray, cut-sides up • Grill for 10 minutes, turning the pieces halfway through cooking, until golden and charred in places

Make the raita • Halve the cucumber lengthways, then remove the watery seeds with a teaspoon and discard • Grate the remaining cucumber into a bowl • Chop the mint and add it to the bowl • Add the coconut yoghurt and mix to combine • Season with salt and black pepper

Heat the breads • Warm or toast the bread in the microwave or a pan • Slice the spring onions

Serve • Spread a spoonful of the raita over each of the breads • Top with the tandoori chick'n • Squeeze a half of grilled lime over each • Finish with coriander leaves and sliced spring onion • Add a pinch of chilli flakes, if using

Mushroom Keema Rice

Big bowls of rice that are bursting with big, punchy flavours are our kind of food: speedy *and* satisfying. This mushroom mince-based dish is perfect as a main with an aromatic side salad and some raita, but it's also great as part of a big curry spread. If you're a fan of an Indian takeaway every now and again, you should definitely make this.

Serves 4

250g basmati rice
500ml boiling water
2 tbsp vegetable oil
500g mushrooms (we used chestnut)
2 tsp garam masala
2 tsp ground turmeric
1 tsp cumin seeds
1 x 400g tin chopped tomatoes
200g frozen peas
1 lime
salt and black pepper

For the spice paste
1 large onion
2 garlic cloves
5cm piece of fresh ginger
1 fresh green chilli
30g fresh coriander

For the cucumber yoghurt
½ cucumber
handful of fresh mint leaves
200g coconut yoghurt
salt and black pepper

Kettle boiled • Microwaveable bowl • Microwave • Clean tea towel • Food processor • Large, deep frying pan or casserole • Grater

Cook the rice • Rinse the rice well with cold water • Tip into a microwaveable bowl and add the boiling water • Microwave on high for 8 minutes • Cover with a tea towel and set aside

Make the spice paste • Peel and roughly chop the onion • Peel the garlic and ginger and trim the chilli • Pick the coriander leaves and reserve them for garnish • Tip the onion, garlic, coriander stems, ginger and chilli into a food processor • Blitz to a rough paste

Make the curry • Put the frying pan or casserole over a medium-high heat • Heat the vegetable oil • Add the curry paste and fry for 3 minutes • Meanwhile, roughly chop the mushrooms • Add the spices to the pan and fry for 1 minute • Tip the mushrooms into the pan and fry for 8 minutes until starting to soften

Make the cucumber yoghurt • Grate the cucumber into a bowl • Roughly chop the mint and add it to the bowl • Add the coconut yoghurt and stir through • Season with salt and pepper

Finish the curry • Add the chopped tomatoes to the pan and stir them through • Simmer for 3 minutes • Add the frozen peas and the cooked rice and stir • Halve the lime and cut one half into wedges • Squeeze the juice from the other half into the curry, stir well and season with salt and pepper

Serve • Scatter the curry with the coriander leaves and serve with the cucumber yoghurt and lime wedges

Cheat's Black Dal

Traditionally, dal is a dish that is cooked for a long time – low and slow. To make it super fast, we're using pre-cooked lentils and kidney beans, and upping the spices and coconut milk. Boom! This is great on its own, or serve it with some chapatis or rice and a sprinkling of fresh coriander.

Serves 4

2 tbsp coconut oil
4 garlic cloves
30g fresh ginger
1 tbsp garam masala
1 tsp ground cumin
5 whole cloves
½–1 tsp chilli powder (to taste)
¾ tsp ground cinnamon
2 bay leaves
2 heaped tbsp tomato purée
300ml water
1 x 400g tin coconut milk
½ x 400g tin kidney beans
2 x 250g pouches cooked
    Beluga lentils
salt and black pepper

To serve
drizzle of coconut milk or
    dairy-free coconut yoghurt
crispy onions
handful of fresh coriander leaves
chapatis or rice

Wide, shallow casserole dish or frying pan over a medium-low heat • Microplane or fine grater • Large jug • Stick blender

Make the base • Heat the coconut oil in the casserole or pan • Crush the garlic cloves and add them to the pan • Grate the ginger directly into the pan • Stir-fry for 1 minute • Add the spices and bay leaves and cook gently for 1 minute • Stir through the tomato purée, 100ml of the water and half the coconut milk • Increase the heat and bring to the boil, stirring from time to time • Reduce the heat to medium and simmer for 8 minutes

Add the lentils and beans • Pour the remaining coconut milk into the jug • Add the kidney beans, a good pinch of salt and pepper, half of one of the lentil pouches and the remaining 200ml of water • Blitz with a stick blender • Add the mixture to the pan and mix well • Bring back to the boil, then reduce to a simmer and cook for a further 6 minutes • Add the remaining lentils to the dal and heat through for 2 more minutes • Season to taste, then remove and discard the bay leaves

Serve • Spoon the dal into bowls and drizzle over coconut milk or yoghurt • Scatter over some crispy onions and coriander leaves • Serve with chapatis or rice

Indonesian Yellow Curry

The paste we developed for this curry gives it a lovely sunny colour and an incredibly zingy flavour. The courgettes give body and the peppers provide bite, while the coconut and lemongrass rice complements the curry perfectly. All in all, this is a really well-rounded, satisfying meal that's perfect for any night of the week.

Serves 2

1 tbsp coconut oil
1 large courgette
1 red pepper
2 limes
black pepper

For the spice paste
1 lemongrass stalk
thumb-sized piece of fresh ginger
1 tsp lazy garlic or 2 garlic
    cloves, crushed
1 tbsp ground turmeric
1 fresh green bird's-eye chilli
2 tbsp coconut oil
2 tsp soy sauce
splash of water

For the rice
100g basmati rice
200ml water
generous pinch of salt
1 x 400g tin coconut milk
1 lemongrass stalk

To serve
handful of fresh coriander
handful of toasted coconut flakes

Small food processor or blender • Small saucepan with lid • Large frying pan • Microplane or fine grater • Sieve • Tea towel • Small frying pan

Make the spice paste • Put all the spice paste ingredients into a small food processor or blender and blitz to a coarse paste • Be careful with the turmeric as it will stain!

Make the rice • Put the rice, water and salt into a small lidded saucepan • Carefully open the tin of coconut milk without shaking it, scoop out the thick coconut cream from the top and set it aside, then pour the milk into the pan • Bash the lemongrass stalk with a rolling pin or the back of knife and add it to the pan • Cover and bring to the boil, then reduce to a simmer and cook for 10 minutes

Meanwhile, make the curry • Set the frying pan over a medium heat • Melt the coconut oil • Add the curry paste and cook until it starts to sizzle • Chop the courgette at an angle into long discs and add to the pan, stirring to coat with the paste • Fry for about 5 minutes until starting to turn golden • Roughly chop the red pepper and add it to the pan • Add the reserved coconut cream and stir through, then leave to cook for 2–3 minutes, until the vegetables are just tender • Zest one of the limes into the pan, then halve it and squeeze in the juice • Cut the remaining lime into 4 wedges and set aside • Season to taste with black pepper

To finish • Holding a sieve over the curry pan, drain the cooked rice over the top of the curry, letting the starchy cooking water enrich the sauce • Discard the lemongrass • Place the rice in the sieve back on top of the rice pan and cover with a tea towel • Put the small frying pan over a medium heat • Sprinkle over the coconut flakes and toast until starting to colour • Take off the heat

Serve • Spoon the rice and curry into bowls and top with coriander and coconut flakes • Serve with the lime wedges

Cheatball Marinara Sub

This is how to make a quick and healthy marinara sub. Choose your favourite type of 'meatballs' and rustle up a super-quick tommie sauce and some vegan cheese. You could even use veggie sausage slices, if you're in a pinch! Depending on the size of sub that you use, you may have a few meatballs left over to reheat for an easy-win meal later on.

Makes 2 large subs

1 onion
½ fennel bulb
½ fresh red chilli
2 tbsp olive oil
½ tsp lazy garlic or
    ½ garlic clove, crushed
1 tsp sweet paprika
8 shop-bought veggie meatballs
1 x 200g tin chopped tomatoes
1 tbsp tomato purée
1 tsp sugar
handful of fresh basil leaves
2 roasted red peppers from a jar

For the cheese sauce
60g dairy-free Cheddar cheese
60ml unsweetened plant-based milk
1 tbsp nutritional yeast
handful of chives
1 tsp English mustard
salt and pepper

To serve
2 sub baguettes, about 30cm each
plant-based butter

Frying pan on a medium heat • Grater • Small saucepan • Whisk

Prepare the meatballs • Peel and finely dice the onion • Finely dice the fennel (including the tops) • Finely chop the chilli (leave the seeds in if you like the heat) • Heat the olive oil in the hot frying pan • Add the onion, fennel and chilli to the pan along with the garlic and paprika and cook, stirring, until starting to soften • Add the veggie meatballs and fry for a couple of minutes • Add the chopped tomatoes, tomato purée, sugar and basil leaves • Slice the roasted pepper and add that too, then leave the mixture to simmer while you make the cheese sauce

Make the cheese sauce • Put the small saucepan over a low heat • Grate the dairy-free cheese • Add the plant-based milk, cheese and nutritional yeast to the saucepan and whisk until thickened • Finely chop the chives and stir them into the sauce along with the mustard • Season with salt and pepper

To serve • Cut open the baguettes and butter them with the plant-based butter • Spoon 4 meatballs into each sub with the tomato sauce, then drizzle over the cheese sauce

Thai Green Curry Bowls

This fragrant dish has hearty tofu and rice, texture from the lovely crunchy veggies and smooth coconut milk, and a great depth of flavour from the vegan Thai green curry paste, which is now easy to find in big supermarkets. Don't worry if some of the rice sticks to the pan a bit – the crispy rice adds extra flavour and texture! It's not the most traditional dish we've ever developed, but it's an absolute winner.

Serves 4

1 tbsp vegetable oil
4 tbsp vegan Thai green curry paste
280g firm or smoked tofu
300g easy cook rice
1 x 400ml tin coconut milk
1 tbsp smooth peanut butter
200g pak choi
200g sugar snap peas
200g baby corn
50g peanuts
bunch of fresh coriander
2 limes
salt and black pepper

Large saucepan or skillet with a lid on a medium heat

Start the curry • Add the oil to the hot pan • Add the curry paste and fry for 1 minute • Cut the tofu into 2cm chunks and add it to the pan • Stir to coat and fry for 1 minute • Rinse and drain the rice and stir it into the pan • Pour in the coconut milk then fill the empty tin with water and add to the pan • Add the peanut butter and a big pinch of salt • Stir well • Increase the heat to high and bring the mixture to a bubble • Reduce the heat to medium

Prepare the veg • Cut the pak choi into halves or quarters • Add to the pan with the sugar snaps and baby corn • Cover with the lid or foil and leave to cook for 7 minutes • Roughly chop the peanuts • Pick the coriander leaves • Slice one lime in half and the other into 4 wedges

Finish the curry • Take the lid off the pan and give it a good stir • Put the lid back on and cook for 5 more minutes until the rice is cooked through • Take off the heat • Squeeze over the juice of the halved lime and stir it through • Taste and season with salt and black pepper

Serve • Spoon the curry into bowls • Top with the lime wedges, coriander leaves and chopped peanuts

Big Red Peanut Noodles

Spicy, aromatic and filling – this dish has got the lot. The red from the chilli, the purple from the red cabbage and the green from the herbs all look great together and taste amazing. When you throw the creamy, salty, spicy peanut sauce into the mix, you get a bowl of noodles that you wish would never end.

Serves 2

1 large aubergine
pinch of salt
¼ red cabbage (about 300g)
handful of fresh coriander
handful of fresh mint leaves
50g roasted and salted peanuts
1 lime
1 fresh red chilli (optional)
100g flat rice noodles
1 tbsp vegetable or sesame oil
1 garlic clove
thumb-sized piece of fresh ginger

For the sauce
1 lime
2 tbsp smooth peanut butter
2 tbsp soy sauce
1 tbsp sweet chilli sauce
1 tbsp water
salt and black pepper

Frying pan over a high heat • Kettle boiled • Whisk • Microplane or fine grater

Start with the aubergine • Chop the aubergine into 1.5cm cubes • Add to the hot frying pan with pinch of salt • Dry-fry for 5–7 minutes until charred and collapsing, tossing regularly

Prepare the other ingredients • Finely slice the red cabbage • Remove the coriander stalks and roughly chop • Chop the leaves of the herbs • Chop the peanuts • Cut the lime in half • Slice the chilli, if using

Cook the noodles • Put the noodles in a bowl and pour over boiling water to cover • Leave to soak according to the packet instructions, until tender

Return to the aubergine • Add the coriander stalks and cabbage to the pan along with the oil • Cook for 2–3 minutes until the cabbage has softened

Drain and rinse the noodles under cold running water • Set aside

Make the sauce • Halve the lime and squeeze the juice into a bowl • Add all the other sauce ingredients and whisk together • Season with salt and pepper

Return to the pan • Peel the garlic • Grate the garlic and ginger directly into the pan • Cook, stirring, for 1 minute • Add the noodles, dressing and most of the herbs to the pan, along with a splash of water • Cook for 1 minute, tossing well so everything is covered in the dressing

Serve • Split the mixture between 2 bowls • Top with the remaining herbs, chopped peanuts and sliced red chilli • Serve with the lime halves for squeezing over

Quick Fried Biryani

If you're after a dish that's packed full of protein, has loads of different textures and is bursting with wonderful flavours, you've turned to the right page. This quick biryani is one of our favourite dishes in this book. If you're a fan of curry and Indian flavours, give it a go – we're sure you'll love it as much as we do!

Serves 2

150g baby potatoes
3 tbsp coconut oil
2 tsp ground turmeric
1 tsp ground cumin
pinch of salt
250g pre-cooked basmati rice
100g pre-cooked Puy lentils
100g frozen peas

For the roast aubergine
1 medium aubergine
1 tsp cumin seeds
1 tsp coriander seeds
1 tbsp vegetable oil
½ tsp garlic powder
1 tbsp garam masala
generous pinch of salt

For the raita
½ cucumber
½ lemon
4 tbsp coconut yoghurt
1 tbsp mint sauce
salt

To serve
handful of fresh coriander
2 spring onions
accompaniments of choice (lime
    pickle, mango chutney, etc.)

Preheat oven to 200°C • Line a baking tray • Medium pan of water on a high heat • Grater • Large frying pan or casserole with a lid

Start with the aubergine • Chop the aubergine into roughly 1cm dice and tumble them onto the lined baking tray • Crush the cumin and coriander seeds and sprinkle them over the top • Drizzle over the vegetable oil • Sprinkle the garlic powder, garam masala and salt over the aubergine and toss to coat • Place on the top shelf of the oven to roast for about 15 minutes

Cook the potatoes • Halve the potatoes and add them to the pan of boiling water • Boil for 10 minutes • Drain and leave to steam dry

Meanwhile, make the raita • Halve the cucumber lengthways, then remove the watery seeds with a teaspoon and discard • Grate the remaining cucumber into a bowl • Juice the lemon half directly into the bowl • Stir in the coconut yoghurt and mint sauce • Add salt to taste

Make the biryani • Put the frying pan or casserole over a medium heat and melt the coconut oil • Tip in the cooked potatoes and add the turmeric, cumin and salt • Stir-fry for 4 minutes • Tip in the rice and lentils and stir-fry for another 2 minutes • Remove the roasted aubergines from the oven, add them to the pan and stir through • Tip in the peas, then cover the pan and reduce the heat to low for the last 3–4 minutes

To serve • Chop the coriander and spring onions • Take 4 wide bowls, the raita and any other accompaniments to the table • Take the lid off the pan and sprinkle over the coriander and spring onions • Take the pan to the table and serve with accompaniments of your choice

Speedy Laksa

Laksa is a beautifully spicy noodle soup that's popular throughout Southeast Asia. We've sped up this wonderful dish by using red curry paste. There are still a good few ingredients, but trust us, you can get through it in under half an hour. It's wonderfully complex and each mouthful has hints of sweet, sour and bitter flavours. BOSH!

Serves 3–4

250g flat rice noodles
1 large sweet potato
1 tbsp sesame oil
1 tsp ground coriander
1 tsp ground turmeric
4 tbsp vegan Thai red curry paste
1 tbsp soft brown sugar
1 x 400ml tin coconut milk
1 litre vegetable stock
200g Tenderstem broccoli
2 limes
4 tbsp soy sauce
100g beansprouts
small handful of fresh coriander leaves
small handful of fresh mint leaves
chilli oil, for drizzling (optional)

For the tofu puffs

1 x 280g block firm tofu
2 tbsp cornflour
2 tbsp sunflower oil
salt and black pepper

Kettle boiled • Microwaveable bowl • Clingfilm • Microwave • Large saucepan on a medium-high heat • Kitchen paper • Large frying pan on a medium-high heat

Cook the noodles • Put the rice noodles in a bowl and cover with boiling water • Leave for about 15 minutes until soft

Cook the sweet potato • Chop the sweet potato into bite-sized chunks and put into a microwaveable bowl • Cover with clingfilm and microwave on high for 7 minutes

Make the soup • Heat the sesame oil in the large saucepan • Add the spices and fry for 1 minute • Add the curry paste and sugar and fry for 2 minutes • Add the coconut milk and stock and bring to the boil • Boil for 5 minutes

Make the tofu puffs • Pat the tofu dry with kitchen paper and chop it into 2cm cubes • Scatter cornflour over the cubes and season with salt and pepper, tossing them until coated • Heat the sunflower oil in the large frying pan • Add the tofu and fry for 3–4 minutes until crisp, tossing regularly

Finish the soup • Cut the top 10cm off the broccoli and finely slice the stems • Slice one of the limes in half and the other into wedges • Add the broccoli stems and tops to the soup • Add the cooked sweet potato and boil for 2 minutes • Squeeze in the juice of the halved lime and add the soy sauce

Build the bowls • Drain and rinse the noodles • Split the noodles between 4 bowls and top each with handful of beansprouts and some of the tofu puffs • Spoon the soup and veg into the bowls • Garnish with coriander and mint leaves • Drizzle with chilli oil, if you like it spicy

Sloppy Joe Dogs

The sloppy joe sandwich is said to have been invented by a chef called Joe at Floyd Angell's café in Sioux City, Iowa – he added tomato sauce to his 'loose meat' sandwich and a new dish was born. Ours is plant-based, obviously, and we've combined our sloppy joe sauce with a vegan hot dog to truly audacious effect! The coke and Marmite give the sauce extra depth which, combined with the zesty pickles and spicy mustard, makes a real treat for the taste buds. These are meant to be messy, embrace it!

Serves 4

4 plant-based sausages
    (tofu frankfurters)

For the sloppy joe sauce
1 x 350g pack plant-based mince
1 x 200g tin chopped tomatoes
275ml cola
125g tomato ketchup
35g Marmite
20–50g hot sauce or chilli sauce
pinch of dried oregano

To serve
4 large hot dog rolls
2 handfuls of lettuce
handful of fresh coriander leaves
4 pinches of ready-made
    crispy onions (or 2 spring
    onions/½ onion)
2–4 tbsp pickled green chillies
    or jalapeños
burger gherkins
American mustard

Preheat grill to medium-high or have a griddle pan ready • Wide heavy-based pan on a medium heat

Make the sauce • Add all the sauce ingredients to the hot pan and stir to combine • Bring to the boil and simmer for about 10 minutes, until reduced by half

Meanwhile, cook the hot dogs • Grill the sausages according to the packet instructions or heat a griddle pan over a medium-high heat and cook them for 2–5 minutes on each side

Assemble • Split each hot dog roll • Chop the lettuce and coriander • Thinly slice the spring onions or onion, if using • Add a layer of lettuce to one side of each roll • Add a base layer of the chopped coriander, crispy or sliced onions, pickles and gherkins • Add a drizzle of mustard, then a spoonful of the sloppy joe sauce • Add the hot dogs, more sloppy joe sauce and more pickles, onions and mustard, to taste

Sticky Sichuan Tofu

Firm tofu, when prepared and cooked properly, is an ingredient that can delight time and time again. Most people just don't know how to cook it properly. In this recipe, we use cornflour to give the tofu a tremendous crunchy texture. The Sichuan sauce is really authentic – sticky, sweet and spicy, exactly like the Sichuan sauce you'd expect to get in a Chinese restaurant. Served with jasmine rice, sesame seeds and a sprinkling of spring onions, this might be the perfect at-home takeaway!

Serves 4

2 x 280g blocks firm tofu
1 tbsp soy sauce
2 tbsp vegetable oil
8 tbsp cornflour
bunch of spring onions
2 x 250g pouches pre-cooked
    jasmine rice
2 limes
2 tbsp sesame seeds
salt and black pepper

For the sauce
1½ tsp Sichuan peppercorns
    (or normal peppercorns
    if you can't find them)
1½ tsp chilli flakes
1 tbsp vegetable oil
1 garlic clove
2cm piece of fresh ginger
4 tbsp soy sauce
3 tbsp maple syrup
2 tbsp rice vinegar or lime juice

Preheat the oven to 220°C • Line a baking tray • Frying pan • Pestle and mortar • Microplane or fine grater • Small frying pan

Prepare the tofu • Cut the tofu into 2cm cubes • Put the soy sauce and 1 tablespoon of the oil in a bowl and mix • Tip the cornflour into a separate bowl and season with salt and pepper • Add the tofu chunks to the soy mixture and toss, then dip and roll in the cornflour to coat the pieces • Spread out on the lined baking tray • Bake in the oven for 15 minutes • Chop all but one of the spring onions into 3cm lengths • When the tofu has been cooking for 5 minutes, take the tray out of the oven and arrange the spring onions around the tofu • Drizzle with 1 tablespoon of the oil • Return to the oven to cook for the remaining 10 minutes, until the tofu is crisp and the spring onions are softened

Meanwhile, make the sauce • Set the frying pan over a high heat • Tip the peppercorns and chilli flakes into the hot pan and toast for 1 minute, then transfer to a pestle and mortar and crush well • Reduce the heat to medium and add the oil • Peel the garlic • Tip the spices back into the pan • Grate the garlic and ginger directly into the pan • Add the rest of the sauce ingredients and bubble over a medium heat until glossy

Prepare the rice • Cook the rice according to the packet instructions and tip it into a bowl • Halve the limes and squeeze the juice of one into the rice • Season well • Slice the other lime into wedges • Slice the final spring onion

Toast the sesame seeds • Put the small frying pan over a medium-high heat • Add the sesame seeds and toast them until golden • Take off the heat and set aside

To finish • Take the tray out of the oven • Set aside the spring onions and tip the crispy tofu into the sauce pan • Stir to coat

To serve • Spoon the rice onto plates and top with the crispy tofu and roasted spring onions • Sprinkle with the toasted sesame seeds and sliced fresh spring onion • Serve with the lime wedges

Potato Chaat with Crispy Chickpeas

Chaat typically refers to the classic Indian street food – snacks just like this – that you'd eat on the streets in Mumbai or Delhi. This potato chaat explodes with textures and flavours. With zingy, crispy chickpeas and gorgeous fresh accompaniments, it works great on its own, but is even better when paired with a curry like our Butter Tofu Curry (see page 105) or Cheat's Black Dal (see page 115).

Serves 4

2 large baking potatoes
2 tbsp vegetable oil
2 tbsp curry powder
salt and black pepper

For the crispy chickpeas
1 tbsp vegetable oil
1 x 400g tin chickpeas
thumb-sized piece of fresh ginger
1 tsp cumin seeds
1 tsp garam masala

To serve
4 roti or dairy-free naan breads
1 x 120g tub coconut yoghurt
2 tbsp mango chutney
1 tbsp water
2 spring onions
small bunch of fresh coriander
1 lime
30g Bombay mix
60g pomegranate seeds
1 tsp chilli flakes (optional)

Large saucepan of salted water on a high heat • Large frying pan on a high heat • Microplane or fine grater

Start with the potatoes • Bring the pan of salted water to the boil • Chop the potatoes into 2cm chunks • Add the potatoes to the pan and cook for 7–8 minutes until soft but not falling apart

Meanwhile, make the crispy chickpeas • Add 1 tablespoon of the oil to the hot frying pan • Drain the chickpeas and shake them well to remove as much liquid as possible • Tip them into the hot oil and fry for 3–4 minutes, until starting to crisp up • Grate the ginger directly into the pan • Add the cumin seeds and garam masala and stir to thoroughly coat the chickpeas in the spices • Tip into a bowl and set aside, keeping the pan for the next step

Drain the potatoes • Add another tablespoon of oil to the frying pan and set it back over a high heat • Add the curry powder and potatoes and toss to coat in the oil • Cook for 8–10 minutes, until starting to crisp up • Season with salt and pepper

Meanwhile, make the accompaniments • Heat the roti or naan in the microwave • Whip the coconut yoghurt • Mix the mango chutney with the water • Slice the spring onions • Pick the coriander leaves • Slice the lime into wedges

Assemble • Tip the potatoes onto a large serving plate and top with the crispy chickpeas • Drizzle the coconut yoghurt over the top, then drizzle over the mango chutney mixture • Scatter with a large handful of Bombay mix, coriander leaves, sliced spring onions, pomegranate seeds and chilli flakes, if using • Serve with the roti or naan for mopping up the juices and the lime wedges on the side

Spicy Dan Dan Noodles

This is perhaps one of the most surprising dishes in this book, a classic Chinese recipe with incredible flavour. It may not be much to look at, but this dish wows the taste buds with its ginger, garlic and 5 spice. The noodles, meanwhile, are great at absorbing flavour and super speedy. Trust us, you'll love this recipe. It's one of Ian's all-time faves.

Serves 2

1 tbsp sesame oil, plus extra if needed
125g mushrooms (we used shiitake)
200g plant-based mince
3 spring onions
200g ramen noodles (or
    whichever noodles you prefer)
2 garlic cloves
thumb-sized piece of fresh ginger
1 tsp Chinese 5 spice
chilli oil, for drizzling
2 tbsp sesame seeds
salt

For the sauce
50ml water
2 tbsp tahini
2 tbsp soy sauce
1 tbsp rice vinegar
    or balsamic vinegar
1 tbsp sesame oil
1 tsp sugar
1 tsp chilli flakes

Large saucepan of salted water on a high heat • Frying pan on a high heat • Microplane or fine grater

Start with the mince • Heat the sesame oil in the hot frying pan • Finely chop the mushrooms and add them to the pan with pinch of salt • Add the mince to the pan and fry for about 10 minutes, stirring regularly, until you are left with a crispy mixture (turn down the heat if you find it sticks to the pan too much) • Slice the spring onions and set aside

Meanwhile, cook the noodles • Add the noodles to the pan of boiling water and cook according to the packet instructions • Drain and rinse with cold water

Make the sauce • Mix together all the sauce ingredients in a bowl

Return to the mince • Peel the garlic and grate it directly into the pan along with the ginger • Add the Chinese 5 spice • Cook for 1 minute, adding a splash more sesame oil if it looks too dry • Pour in a third of the sauce and cook for 2 minutes until the mince is slightly browned • Remove half the mince mixture and set it aside • Reduce the heat to low while the noodles finish cooking • Transfer the cooked noodles to the pan and add most of the spring onion, keeping a handful back for garnish • Increase the heat, pour in the remaining sauce and stir well, adding a splash of water to loosen if necessary

Serve • Divide the noodle mixture between 2 bowls • Top with the reserved crispy mince • Finish each portion with a drizzle of chilli oil, sesame seeds and the remaining spring onion

Sharing

03

BBQ Tempeh Ribs

Tempeh is an ingredient that, up until a couple of years ago, you'd only have been able to find in health food shops. With the recent explosion in popularity of vegan food, it's now a lot easier to get hold of. If you've never tried it before, this recipe must be the first tempeh dish you try! It's truly incredible, and so, so easy… The tempeh ribs are sticky, sweet and tangy, the corn is rich and creamy, and the pecan slaw is fresh and crunchy. This is the kind of meal you'll be thinking about for days after you eat it.

Serves 2

200g tempeh
6 tbsp shop-bought BBQ sauce
2 tbsp red wine vinegar
1 tsp fennel seeds
pinch of salt

For the creamed corn
100g sweetcorn (from
    the cob or tinned)
70ml soya cream
½ tsp smoked paprika
pinch of salt

For the slaw
handful of pecans
1½ tsp maple syrup
pinch of salt
¼ red cabbage
¼ sweetheart/white cabbage
¼ lime

To serve
2 spring onions

Preheat grill to high • Large saucepan of water on a high heat • Steamer pan or colander • Line a baking tray • Large ramekin • Small frying pan

Make the ribs • Tip the tempeh into the boiling water and blanch for 3 minutes • Put the BBQ sauce, red wine vinegar, fennel seeds and salt into a mixing bowl and mix well • Remove the tempeh from the pan and cut it into finger-sized strips • Add them to the sauce and toss to coat • Arrange the tempeh on the lined baking tray, leaving some of the marinade behind in the bowl for later • Put under the grill for 5 minutes (if they start to bubble and brown, baste with some of the reserved marinade and give them a turn)

Meanwhile, make the creamed corn • Rinse the corn • Place the kernels in a large ramekin along with the soya cream and sprinkle over the smoked paprika and salt • Slide under the grill next to the tempeh ribs

Make the slaw • Set the frying pan over a medium heat • Add the pecans, maple syrup and salt and toss to coat the pecans in the syrup • Jiggle the pan a few times to stop the pecans burning • Fry until caramelised and sticky • Thinly slice the cabbages and put them into a salad bowl • Squeeze over the juice of the lime and top with the caramelised pecans

Serve • Once the ribs are nicely browned and the corn is bubbling and brown on top, carefully remove from the grill • Brush the ribs with the remaining marinade • Slice the spring onions and scatter them over the ribs • Take everything to the table with the slaw and plenty of napkins!

MUHAMMARA

BEETROOT,
TAHINI &
DILL DIP

PEA,
FETA &
MINT DIP

Quick Mezze Platter

Perfect for entertaining, nibbling or eating for lunch at your desk, little mezze dips are a weekly staple in the BOSH! household. We've combined some newly discovered flavours with a few classics, and for the full Levantine effect we've matched the dips with flatbreads, shop-bought dolmades and dippy veg. You'll definitely need a food processor here and, if you're making them all, having a silicone spatula to hand would be very helpful to speed up the process.

Serves 4–6

Pea, Feta & Mint Dip
  (see page 144)
Beetroot, Tahini & Dill Dip
  (see opposite)
Muhammara (see opposite)
Crudités, Dolmades, Pickled
  Chillies & Flatbreads
  (see page 144)

Preheat grill to high • Food processor

Remove the peas for the **Pea, Feta & Mint Dip** from the freezer and set aside to thaw slightly until needed

Next, make the **Beetroot, Tahini & Dill Dip**

Now make the **Muhammara**

Assemble the **Pea, Feta & Mint Dip**

Prepare the **Crudités, Dolmades, Pickled Chillies & Flatbreads**

Serve • Bring everything to the table and let your guests tuck in!

Beetroot, Tahini & Dill Dip

Serves 4–6

½ lime
2 cooked beetroot
2 tbsp tahini
a small handful of dill
½ tsp sesame seeds
salt

Food processor

Squeeze the lime juice into the food processor • Add the beetroot, tahini and a generous sprinkling of salt • Blitz until smooth • Check the seasoning and adjust if necessary • Scrape the dip into a serving bowl • Roughly chop the feathery fronds of the dill and sprinkle them over the dip along with the sesame seeds

Muhammara

Serves 4–6

½ lemon
1 roasted red pepper from a jar
2 tbsp pomegranate molasses
½ tsp chilli flakes
½ tsp ground cumin
2 tbsp olive oil
1 tsp salt
80g walnuts

For the topping
10g walnuts
handful of fresh flat-leaf parsley

Food processor

Squeeze the juice of the lemon half into the food processor • Add all the rest of the muhammara ingredients and blitz until smooth • Scrape into a serving bowl • Chop the walnuts and sprinkle them over the dip, then garnish with the parsley leaves

Pea, Feta & Mint Dip

Serves 4–6

½ lemon
80g frozen petit pois
100g dairy-free feta
3 tbsp rapeseed oil
handful of fresh mint leaves

For the topping
1 tbsp olive oil
small handful of fresh mint leaves

Food processor

Squeeze the lemon juice into the food processor • Add the slightly thawed petit pois, feta, oil and mint leaves • Blitz until well combined, but still retaining some texture • Scrape into a serving bowl and swirl the top with the back of a spoon to make a small indent • Drizzle the olive oil into the dip and garnish with mint leaves

Crudités, Dolmades, Pickled Chillies & Flatbreads

Serves 4–6

6 flatbreads
1 carrot
½ cucumber
½ fennel bulb
6 celery sticks
a bunch of radishes
    with leaves
pinch of dried mint
½ lemon
1 x 300g jar pickled
    green chillies
1 x 280g tin dolmades

Preheat grill to high

Toast the flatbreads under the hot grill for 1–2 minutes • Trim and slice the carrot, cucumber, fennel and celery into sticks or wedges for dipping • Rinse and halve the radishes, retaining their leaves • Arrange the vegetables on a platter, sprinkle over the dried mint and squeeze over a little lemon juice • Drain the pickled chillies and dolmades and transfer to small serving dishes

Chimichurri Seitan Fajitas

A trusty food processor helps you whizz this delicious green spicy salsa up faster than you can say 'Fajita'! Chimichurri is basically an Argentinian version of salsa verde, packed with fresh herbs, zingy flavour and muchos deliciousness. Shredded strips of seitan (wheat protein – delish) have a similar texture to steak and sizzle up a treat in the pan. Add your classic fajita accoutrements and you've got a right old wrap. Oof!

Serves 4

For the chimichurri
3 spring onions
handful of flat-leaf parsley
handful of fresh coriander
½ fresh green chilli
1 tsp dried oregano
½ tsp lazy garlic or
    ½ garlic clove, crushed
large pinch of salt
2 tbsp red wine vinegar
1 tsp agave or maple syrup
1 tsp olive oil

For the seitan
175g seitan steaks
1 onion
1 yellow pepper
1 tbsp vegetable oil

For the sour cream
4 tbsp dairy-free cream cheese
½ lime
pinch of salt
1 spring onion

For the salsa
4 medium tomatoes
1 shallot
handful of coriander stalks
pinch of salt
½ tsp smoked paprika
½ lime

To serve
1 little gem lettuce
2 roasted red peppers from a jar
1 ripe avocado
1 lime
4 large tortilla wraps

Food processor • Frying pan

Make the chimichurri • Trim the spring onions • Place all the chimichurri ingredients in the food processor and blitz to a coarse sauce • Place half in a bowl and set aside

Make the seitan • Slice the seitan into strips and toss it in a bowl with the other half of the chimichurri • Peel and slice the onion • Slice the yellow pepper • Set the frying pan over a medium heat and heat the oil • Fry the seitan for 5 minutes • Add the onion and pepper and continue to fry, stirring so it doesn't burn (although a bit of blackening is good), until the veg is soft

Prep the sour cream • Mix the dairy-free cream cheese, lime juice and salt in a bowl • Finely chop the spring onion and sprinkle it on top

Prep the salsa • Roughly chop the tomatoes, discarding as many of the seeds as you can, and place in a bowl • Peel and finely slice the shallot • Chop the coriander stalks • Add to the bowl with the salt and smoked paprika • Mix vigorously with clean hands or a wooden spoon in order to bruise everything to release the flavour and juices • Squeeze in the juice of the lime and stir again

To serve • Slice the lettuce and peppers • Peel and slice the avocado • Cut the lime into quarters • Take everything to the table with the bowl of chimichurri • Give everyone a plate with a tortilla wrap • Bring the pan of seitan to the table and let everyone assemble their own fajitas

Naan Tikka Pizza

Curry? Good. Pizza? Good. Speed? **Good.** What's not to like? These naan pizzas are the perfect things to rustle up for lunch on a Saturday or if you're working from home during the week. The sweet potatoes are healthy and filling and the coriander chutney has a really lovely zippy flavour that's sure to put a smile on your face. But the real punch comes from the curry paste and yoghurt, combining to give you all the wonderful flavours of a curry, but with the convenience of a slice of toast. Get involved!

Serves 4

2 large sweet potatoes (about 800g)
2 tbsp tikka curry paste
1 tbsp vegetable oil
150g Tenderstem broccoli
4 dairy-free naans or thick
   flatbreads
200ml coconut yoghurt
4 tbsp mango chutney
1 tbsp black onion seeds
1 lime

For the coriander chutney
1 lime
1 garlic clove
1 fresh green chilli
small bunch of fresh mint
small bunch of fresh coriander
5cm piece of fresh ginger
2 tbsp vegetable oil
salt and black pepper

Preheat oven to 220°C • Microwaveable bowl • Clingfilm • Microwave • Food processor • Line a baking tray

Cook the sweet potato • Cut the sweet potatoes into bite-sized chunks • Tip into the microwaveable bowl, cover with clingfilm and microwave on high for 8–10 minutes until soft

Make the chutney • Halve the lime and squeeze the juice into the food processor • Peel the garlic • Deseed the chilli if you don't like too much heat • Pick the leaves from the herbs, setting some aside for garnish (keep the coriander stems but discard the mint stems) • Add the garlic, chilli, herb leaves and all the remaining chutney ingredients to the food processor, including the coriander stems • Blitz to a pouring consistency • Season with salt and pepper

Finish the topping • Remove the sweet potatoes from the microwave and discard the clingfilm • Add the tikka curry paste and oil to the bowl • Roughly chop the broccoli and add it to the bowl • Toss everything together and tip onto the baking tray • Place in the hot oven • Put the naan or flatbreads onto another shelf in the oven • Heat through for 5 minutes

Assemble • Spread each of the breads with coconut yoghurt • Top each one with the tikka sweet potato and broccoli mixture • Drizzle with the coriander chutney • Add a few dollops of mango chutney • Scatter with the reserved herbs and some black onion seeds • Slice the lime into wedges and serve on the side

Spicy Stuffed Aubergines

A cheeky twist on the classic dish *Imam Biyaldi*, these stuffed aubergines are to die for. *Imam Biyaldi* roughly translates to 'The priest fainted', and folklore tells us that a priest was so impressed by the dish upon first eating it that he swooned. Our version is definitely delicious enough to make a holy man topple... The mince and onion stuffing browns brilliantly and packs a spicy punch, while the traditional tahini and mint dressing cools the whole thing down.

Serves 2

2 aubergines
2 tbsp harissa paste
handful of flaked almonds
1 fresh red chilli
handful of fresh mint
handful of fresh coriander
80g pomegranate seeds
salt

For the stuffing

2 tbsp olive oil
½ onion
200g plant-based mince
2 tsp ground cinnamon
2 tsp ground coriander
2 tsp ground cumin

For the tahini dressing

100g tahini
1 tbsp dried mint
100ml water
1 lemon
salt

Preheat grill to max • Line a baking tray • Frying pan on a medium heat • Kettle boiled • Whisk

Grill the aubergine • Cut the aubergines in half lengthways and lay them flesh-side up on the baking tray • Score the flesh in a criss-cross pattern, being careful not to pierce the skin • Brush the scored flesh with the harissa paste and sprinkle with salt • Place under the hot grill to cook until soft, about 13–15 minutes

Meanwhile, cook the stuffing mixture • Add the olive oil to the hot frying pan • Peel and dice the onion and add it to the pan • Cook for 4 minutes until soft • Add the mince and the ground spices to the onions and cook until golden and fragrant • Season to taste

Make the dressing • Combine the tahini, mint and water in a bowl • Cut the lemon in half and squeeze in the juice • Whisk to a pouring consistency, adding extra tahini if the mixture is too loose, or extra water if it's too thick • Taste and season with a little salt, if needed

Serve • Take the tray out of the oven and transfer the aubergines to a serving dish • Tip the flaked almonds onto the tray and toast very briefly under the grill • Finely slice the chilli and tear the leaves from the fresh herbs • Tip the spiced stuffing mixture over the aubergines • Drizzle with the tahini dressing • Scatter over the herbs, chilli, pomegranate seeds and toasted flaked almonds, then serve

Street Food Tacos – 3 Ways

Tacos are the perfect things to make for you and your pals. They are a really fun, communal food that always get the conversation flowing. Here's a tasty trio of taco recipes that are absolutely guaranteed to get your party started.

Indonesian Cauliflower Tacos

Makes 8

8 small soft corn tortillas

For the red cabbage sambal
¼ head red cabbage
½ red onion
½ lime
a large pinch of salt
1 tbsp red wine vinegar
1 tbsp desiccated coconut
1 tsp caster sugar
1 fresh red bird's-eye chilli

For the cauliflower
1 head cauliflower
2 tbsp Indonesian yellow curry paste
40ml boiling water
4 tbsp cornflour
60g panko breadcrumbs
100ml water
8 tbsp vegetable oil
pinch of salt

To serve
chilli jam
handful of fresh coriander leaves
2 limes

Preheat grill to medium-high or have an extra frying pan ready • Kettle boiled • Frying pan • Line a baking tray with kitchen paper

Make the sambal • Finely slice the red cabbage and red onion and put in a bowl • Squeeze in the juice of the lime • Add the salt and red wine vinegar and mix well • Add the coconut and sugar • Finely chop the chilli (removing the seeds if you want less heat), add to the bowl and mix again • Set aside

Prepare the cauliflower • Put the curry paste and boiling water into a bowl and whisk to a paste • Put the cornflour in another bowl • Put the panko breadcrumbs in a third bowl • Add the cold water to a fourth bowl • Separate the florets from the cauliflower and toss them in the cornflour • Working quickly, pick up each piece of cauliflower and dip it into the curry paste, then the panko breadcrumbs, then into the water and back into the breadcrumbs • Transfer to a large plate

Cook the cauliflower • Add the oil to the frying pan and place on a medium heat • Fry the cauliflower for 3-4 minutes, turning occasionally until crisp • Transfer to the kitchen paper to drain • Sprinkle with salt

Serve • Warm the tortillas under the grill or in a dry frying pan • Top each taco with the red cabbage sambal, cauliflower, a dollop of chilli jam and some coriander leaves • Slice the limes into wedges and serve alongside

King Oyster Mushroom Tacos

Makes 8

8 small soft corn tortillas

Preheat grill to medium-high or have an extra frying pan ready • Frying pan

Pickle the onions • Peel and finely slice the red onions and put them in a bowl • Add the red wine vinegar, salt and sugar and toss to combine, squeezing the onions firmly between your fingers • Set aside

For the pink pickled onions
2 red onions
6 tbsp red wine vinegar
generous pinch of salt
generous pinch of sugar

For the spiced mushrooms
300g king oyster mushrooms
2 tbsp plant-based butter
2 tsp vegetable oil
2 tbsp fajita spice mix

For the chipotle mayo
2 tbsp egg-free mayonnaise
2 tsp chipotle paste
1 lime
salt

To serve
large handful of crunchy
    lettuce leaves
1 lime

Make the spiced mushrooms • Thickly slice the mushrooms • Put the plant-based butter and vegetable oil in the frying pan and set it over a medium heat • Add the fajita spice mix and mushrooms to the hot pan, stir to coat and fry for about 5 minutes until darkened

For the chipotle mayo • Add the mayo and chipotle paste to a small bowl • Squeeze in the juice of the lime • Mix everything together, adding salt to taste

Serve • Warm the tortillas under the hot grill or in a dry frying pan • Slice the lettuce and fill each taco with a handful • Top each taco with mushrooms, pink pickled onions and chipotle mayo • Slice the lime into wedges and serve alongside

Tartare Sauce Fysh Tacos

Makes 8

8 small soft corn tortillas

For the pink pickled onions
2 red onions
6 tbsp red wine vinegar
generous pinch of salt
generous pinch of sugar

For the fysh
8 frozen fysh fingers

For the tartare sauce
8 cornichons
2 sprigs of fresh dill
1 lemon
3 tbsp egg-free mayonnaise
2 tsp capers
pinch of salt

To serve
large handful of crunchy
    lettuce leaves
2 limes
pinch of salt

Preheat grill to medium-high • Line a baking tray with wet baking paper

Pickle the onions • Peel and finely slice the red onions and put them in a bowl • Add the red wine vinegar, salt and sugar and toss to combine, squeezing the onions firmly between your fingers • Set aside

Prepare the fysh • Place the fysh fingers on the baking tray, put under the grill and cook according to the packet instructions

Make the tartare sauce • Chop the cornichons and dill sprigs and put them in a bowl, saving a few of the dill fronds to garnish • Halve the lemon and squeeze the juice into the bowl • Add the rest of the sauce ingredients and mix well

Serve • Warm the tortillas under the grill or in a dry frying pan • Finely slice the lettuce • Cut the limes into wedges • Put the lettuce in a bowl and dress with a squeeze of lime and some salt • Pile the tacos with lettuce and top with the fysh fingers, pink pickled onions and tartare sauce • Garnish with the reserved dill • Serve with the lime wedges alongside • Feel free to add any other garnishes you fancy, such as your favourite chilli sauces and chutneys

KING OYSTER
MUSHROOM
TACOS

TARTARE
SAUCE FYSH
TACOS

INDONESIAN
CAULIFLOWER
TACOS

Vietnamese Crispy Pancakes

Southeast Asia really is a hotbed of wonderful food. The varied textures, incredible freshness and punchy flavours are all reasons why we love dishes from the region. These Vietnamese crispy pancakes make one of the most impressive-looking dishes we've ever developed – seldom does home-cooked food look this good. If you want to make something that's going to impress your mates and fill you with pride, you have to give these a try. Make sure your frying pan for the pancakes is very non-stick, otherwise the batter can catch on the bottom of the pan.

Makes 4

50g plain flour
50g rice flour
1½ tsp ground turmeric
1 tsp salt
135ml coconut milk
165ml sparkling water

For the mushrooms
250g mushrooms (use shiitake
    if you can find them)
50ml sesame oil
pinch of salt
200g beansprouts
1 tbsp soy sauce
salt and black pepper

For the salad
2 carrots
handful of fresh coriander
handful of fresh basil
handful of fresh mint
1 lime
salt and black pepper

To serve
sweet chilli sauce

2 large frying pans • Whisk • Baking paper • Clean tea towel

Cook the mushrooms • Roughly chop the mushrooms • Put 1 tablespoon of the sesame oil in a frying pan and set it over a high heat • Add the mushrooms and a pinch of salt and fry, stirring occasionally

Make the pancake batter • Put the flours, turmeric and salt into a bowl and mix to combine • Add the coconut milk and sparkling water and whisk to the consistency of double cream • Set aside for 5 minutes

Return to the mushrooms • Add the beansprouts and soy sauce to the pan and toss together for a minute • Season to taste • Set aside

Make the salad • Cut the carrot into ribbons using a vegetable peeler and add to a bowl • Pick the herbs and add the leaves to the bowl • Halve the lime and squeeze over the juice • Toss to combine • Season to taste

Cook the pancakes • Add the rest of the sesame oil to the second frying pan and set it over a medium-high heat • Pour a quarter of the pancake batter into the hot oil and tilt the pan in a circular motion to spread the batter right to the edges • Cook for 2–3 minutes, until the edges of the pancake are crisp • Transfer to a plate and place a sheet of baking paper then a clean tea towel on top • Repeat to make 4 pancakes, layering baking paper between each one

Serve • Place each pancake on a serving plate • Add a quarter of the mushroom mixture to one half of each pancake, along with handful of the carrot and herb salad and fold over • Serve with sweet chilli sauce

Speedy Pizza – 3 Ways

Pizza's good, but speedy pizza is better. Now that ready-made pizza dough is available in UK stores, we've taken to using it regularly. It's a really nice, quick way to make pizza that's almost as good as pizza from a pizzeria at home. Make sure your oven is really hot before you start, it'll really help the cooking process. And trust us, these three toppings are incredible. Henry's fave is the 'nduja, Ian's fave is the broccoli. Enjoy!

Artichoke 'Nduja Pizza

Makes 1 x 12-inch pizza (serves 1–2)

1 x 220g ball shop-bought
    pizza dough
5 tbsp passata
2 tbsp olive oil
handful of fresh basil
plain flour, for dusting

For the 'nduja
1 x 280g jar chargrilled
    artichoke hearts
1 lemon
3 sundried tomatoes
1 roasted red pepper
1 tbsp miso paste
1 tbsp hot smoked paprika
salt and black pepper

This makes more 'nduja than you will need for this recipe, but you can keep it in an airtight container in the fridge for up to a week to use again – it's great on toast!

Defrost dough, if necessary • **Preheat oven to max** • **Put a baking sheet in the oven to heat up** • **Large frying pan on a high heat** • **Food processor** • **Rolling pin**

Make the 'nduja • Tip the artichokes along with 50ml oil from the jar into the hot frying pan • Fry for 2–3 minutes • Slice the lemon in half and squeeze the juice into a food processor • Tip the fried artichokes into the processor with the remaining 'nduja ingredients • Blitz until smooth • Season with salt and pepper

Build the pizza • Dust the work surface with a little of the flour and roll the dough out to a large circle, roughly 25–30cm in diameter • Remove the baking sheet from the oven and scatter with a little more flour • Carefully transfer the pizza base to the hot tray • Spoon the passata onto the dough base and spread out with the back of a spoon • Add dollops of the 'nduja mixture • Put in the oven and cook for 10 minutes

To finish • Remove the pizza from the oven • Drizzle with the olive oil and scatter with the basil

BROCCOLI
& SAUSAGE
PIZZA

ARTICHOKE
NDUJA PIZZA

TEX-MEX
PIZZA

Tex-Mex Pizza

Makes 1 x 12-inch pizza (serving 1–2)

2 roasted red peppers
1 tbsp fajita seasoning
3 tbsp sweetcorn
1 tbsp olive oil
1 x 220g ball shop-bought
    pizza dough
5 tbsp passata
1 avocado
handful of fresh coriander
salt and black pepper
plain flour, for dusting

To serve
hot sauce (optional)

Defrost dough, if necessary • Preheat oven to max • Put a baking sheet in the oven to heat up • Rolling pin

Start with the topping • Slice the roasted peppers into strips and tip them into a mixing bowl • Add the fajita seasoning, sweetcorn and olive oil and toss together • Season with salt and pepper

Build the pizza • Dust the work surface with a little flour • Roll the dough out to a large circle, roughly 25–30cm in diameter • Remove the baking sheet from the oven and scatter with a little more flour • Carefully transfer the pizza base to the hot tray • Spoon the passata onto the dough base and spread it out with the back of a spoon • Spread the topping mixture over the pizza • Put it in the oven to cook for 10 minutes

To finish • Halve and carefully stone the avocado • Remove the flesh and slice • Remove the pizza from the oven • Top with the avocado and fresh coriander • Drizzle with hot sauce, if using

Broccoli & Sausage Pizza

Makes 1 x 12-inch pizza (serving 1–2)

150g long-stem broccoli
4 plant-based sausages
3 tbsp olive oil
½ tsp fennel seeds
pinch of chilli flakes
1 garlic clove
1 x 220g ball shop-bought
    pizza dough
2 tbsp dairy-free crème fraîche
handful of flat-leaf parsley
flour, for dusting

Defrost dough, if necessary • Preheat oven to max • Put a baking sheet in the oven to heat up • Large frying pan over a medium-high heat • Microplane or fine grater • Rolling pin

Start with the topping • Cut off any woody ends from the broccoli • Slice the plant-based sausages • Heat 1 tablespoon of the olive oil in the hot frying pan • Add the sausage slices and fry for 5 minutes, until turning golden • Add the fennel seeds and chilli flakes • Peel and grate the garlic directly into the pan and fry for 2 minutes • Add the broccoli along with another tablespoon of olive oil • Toss to combine

Build the pizza • Dust the work surface with a little flour • Roll the dough out to a large circle, roughly 25–30cm in diameter • Remove the baking sheet from the oven and scatter with a little more flour • Carefully transfer the pizza base to the hot tray • Spread the dairy-free crème fraîche over the base • Spread the sausage and broccoli topping on top • Put in the oven to cook for 10 minutes

To finish • Remove the pizza from the oven • Drizzle with the remaining olive oil and scatter with fresh parsley

Speedy Tapas Platter

This spread is super-quick and tasty! You need lots of pans on the go at once, so it's best to be organised and have all the ingredients ready and to hand. Using the aquafaba from the chickpeas for your tortilla is also a brilliant, waste-free use of ingredients. Try to get good-quality Spanish jarred chickpeas (garbanzos), if you can find them. Most Spanish delis and large supermarkets sell them. This spread is perfect for a hot summer's day, sat in the garden with a jug of our Rosé Sangria (see page 244).

Serves 4–6

Catalan Spinach, Chickpeas
    & Garlic (see page 165)
Quick Tortilla (see page 164)
Padrón Peppers (see page 164)
Marinated Olives & Almonds
    (see page 165)

Preheat oven to a low warming heat • Sieve • 2 mixing bowls • 2 frying pans • Heatproof bowl • Microplane or fine grater

Drain the chickpeas for the Catalan Spinach, Chickpeas & Garlic • Drain the chickpeas, reserving the liquid (aquafaba) • Set aside

Start by cooking the **Quick Tortilla**

While the tortilla is cooking, start the **Padrón Peppers**

Keep the peppers warm in the oven while you make the **Marinated Olives & Almonds**

Finally, make the **Catalan Spinach, Chickpeas & Garlic**

To serve • Bring the dishes to the table for your guests to pick and choose from

Quick Tortilla

Makes 1 large tortilla

handful of flat-leaf parsley
300g aquafaba from 2 x 400g
    tins chickpeas (see Catalan
    Spinach, Chickpeas & Garlic
    recipe, right)
6 tbsp gram or plain flour
1 tbsp smoked paprika
handful of pre-grated
    dairy-free cheese
120g thick crinkle-cut crisps
    (any flavour)
2 tbsp vegetable oil
1 red pepper

Frying pan on a medium-low heat

Prepare the tortilla • Chop the stalks from the parsley and set the leaves aside • Put the aquafaba, flour, smoked paprika, dairy-free cheese and chopped parsley stalks into a bowl • Mix to a smooth paste • Tip in the crisps and carefully mix until coated

Cook the tortilla • Heat the vegetable oil in the hot frying pan • Finely slice the pepper • Tip into the pan and fry for a few minutes, until softened • Tip in the tortilla mixture and flatten with a spatula • Cook for 5–6 minutes until well browned on the bottom and solid enough to flip • Flip, then cook until well browned on the other side and cooked through

Serve • Carefully place a serving plate upside down over the pan and flip the pan, with the plate, so that the tortilla drops onto the plate • Serve with the reserved parsley leaves sprinkled on top

Padrón Peppers

Makes 100g

1 tbsp Spanish olive oil,
    plus extra for drizzling
100g Padrón peppers
sea salt

Preheat oven to 140°C • Frying pan on a high heat • Heatproof bowl

Cook the peppers • Heat the oil in the hot frying pan • Put the peppers in the hot pan with pinch of salt and let them blacken and blister, turning them occasionally • Transfer the peppers to a heatproof bowl and keep warm in the oven on the lowest shelf until ready to serve

Serve • Remove the peppers from the oven and place on a serving plate • Sprinkle with some more sea salt and drizzle with olive oil

Marinated Olives & Almonds

Makes 240g

80g skin-on almonds
pinch of salt
1 tsp dried chilli flakes
150g high-quality green olives
½ lemon
½ orange
Spanish olive oil, for drizzling

Frying pan (the same one you used to cook the Padrón Peppers) on a low heat • Microplane or fine grater

Cook the almonds • Put the almonds in the hot frying pan with the salt, chilli flakes, and a drizzle of oil • Fry until lightly browned

To finish • Drain the olives and put them in a serving bowl • Tip over the almonds and toss together • Zest over the lemon and orange and squeeze over a little juice from each • Add another drizzle of olive oil and take to the table to serve

Catalan Spinach, Chickpeas & Garlic

Makes about 500g

4 tbsp olive oil
3 garlic cloves
2 x 400g tins chickpeas
1 tsp tomato purée
pinch of cayenne pepper
1 tsp smoked paprika
1 tsp ground cumin
3 handfuls fresh baby spinach
1 lemon
salt and black pepper

Frying pan (the same one you used to cook the Padrón Peppers and almonds) on a medium heat

Cook the chickpeas • Add the olive oil to the hot pan • Peel and slice the garlic cloves and add them to the hot oil • When the garlic is sizzling, add the drained chickpeas, turn up the heat and stir for a few minutes until well heated through • Add the tomato purée, cayenne pepper, smoked paprika and ground cumin • Stir to mix the spices with the chickpeas • Add the spinach and stir over the heat while the leaves wilt • Halve the lemon and squeeze in the juice • Add a generous pinch of salt and pepper to taste • Reduce the heat to low until you are ready to serve

Serve • Tip into a serving bowl and serve

Tofu Satay Kebabs with Fresh Herbs

We've both fallen in love with Thailand and its incredible food. The peanutty deliciousness of satay sauce is one of the cornerstones of Thai cooking. Firm tofu is a great partner for it; it's packed full of protein, has a robust texture and takes on flavour beautifully. The marinade for this recipe is both sharp and spicy, while the cornflour coating offers up a cracking crunch.

Serves 4

280g firm tofu
½ lime
2 tbsp tamari/dark soy sauce
2 tbsp sriracha
4 tbsp cornflour
2 tbsp coconut oil

For the satay sauce

1 lime
2 tbsp water
3 tbsp crunchy peanut butter
1 tbsp soy sauce
1 tsp sriracha
1 tsp Chinese vinegar

To serve

2 limes
2 heads of little gem lettuce
4 spring onions
small handful of fresh coriander
small handful of fresh mint
small handful of fresh Thai basil
handful of dry roasted peanuts
1 fresh red chilli
sea salt

Medium frying pan on a medium heat • **Line a plate with kitchen paper** • **Small food processor** • **Mortar and pestle or rolling pin**

Start with the tofu • Slice the tofu into 12 fingers and place in a bowl • Squeeze the lime half over the tofu, then sprinkle over the tamari or soy sauce, sriracha and cornflour and toss to coat • Add the coconut oil to the hot frying pan • Transfer the tofu fingers to the hot oil and fry on all sides until golden • Remove to drain on the kitchen paper

Meanwhile, make the satay sauce • Cut the lime in half and squeeze the juice into the food processor • Add the rest of the sauce ingredients and blitz until smooth • Transfer to a serving bowl

Prepare the wraps and garnishes • Cut the limes into small wedges • Separate the lettuce leaves and arrange them on a serving platter • Sprinkle with a pinch of sea salt and a squeeze of lime from one of the wedges • Snip the spring onions over the lettuce • Arrange the fresh herbs and lime wedges around the platter • Bash the peanuts in a mortar and pestle or with a rolling pin and put them in a serving bowl • Transfer the tofu to a serving plate • Finely chop the chilli and scatter it over the tofu

To serve • Bring everything to the table and let everyone assemble their wraps as they like • Tuck in!

Rainbow Falafel

The mighty falafel is an absolute staple of plant-based eating. In this rainbow recipe, we've created four fabulous falafel flavours, each one a different colour. It's easy to make one of these flavours in less than 30 minutes, but if you're cooking for a crowd, you can make all four pretty quickly too. These are wonderful served with hummus or any of the other dips in this book, but our favourite way is with a garlic tahini dip, so we've thrown in the recipe for that, too!

Falafel Base Mix

Makes 12 falafel of
your chosen flavour

1 garlic clove
150g chickpeas (drained weight)
25g gram flour
½ tsp salt
½ tsp ground cumin
8g fresh parsley

Large food processor

Make the base falafel mix • Peel the garlic clove and add it to the food processor along with the chickpeas, gram flour, salt, ground cumin and parsley, stalks and all • Blitz until smooth

Mix with your falafel purée of choice and cook according to the recipes (pages 171–2)

Tahini & Garlic Dipping Sauce

Makes enough for 12–24 falafel

1 small garlic bulb
1 lemon
3 tbsp tahini
½ tsp salt
pinch of sumac

Garlic crusher • Whisk

Make the sauce • Separate and peel the garlic cloves and crush them into a bowl • Halve the lemon and squeeze the juice into the bowl • Add the rest of the ingredients • Whisk everything together until well combined

Green Falafel

Makes 12 falafel

100g frozen peas
30g fresh spinach
15g fresh mint
1 x quantity Falafel Base Mix
    (see opposite)
vegetable oil, for deep-frying

Large food processor • Large saucepan • Line a tray with kitchen paper

Make the green pea purée • Rinse your peas under the warm tap to quickly defrost, then add to the food processor with the spinach and fresh mint, stalks and all • Blitz until smooth • Scrape the mixture into a large bowl along with the falafel base mix and stir until well combined

Fry your falafel • Pour the vegetable oil into the saucepan so that it comes no more than two-thirds up the sides of the pan • Set over a high heat • Dip a wooden spoon into the oil and if bubbles form around the spoon, you're ready to cook • Carefully scoop tablespoonfuls of falafel mix into the pan (you may need to do this in batches) • Fry, carefully turning the falafel with a slotted spoon, for about 5 minutes, until golden brown all over • Remove to drain on the kitchen paper

Squash Falafel

Makes 12 falafel

140g butternut squash
pinch of salt
15g fresh coriander
1 x quantity Falafel Base Mix
    (see opposite)
vegetable oil, for deep-frying

Microwavable bowl • Clingfilm • Microwave • Large food processor • Large saucepan • Line a tray with kitchen paper

Microwave the squash • Peel and cut the squash into 1½cm cubes • Tip into a microwaveable bowl, cover with clingfilm and microwave on high for 5 minutes

Make the squash purée • Tip the cooked squash, salt and coriander, stalks and all, into the food processor • Blitz until smooth • Scrape the mixture into a large bowl along with the falafel base mix and stir until well combined

Fry your falafel • Pour the vegetable oil into the saucepan so that it comes no more than two-thirds up the sides of the pan • Set over a high heat • Dip a wooden spoon into the oil and if bubbles form around the spoon, you're ready to cook • Carefully scoop tablespoonfuls of falafel mix into the pan (you may need to do this in batches) • Fry, carefully turning the falafel with a slotted spoon, for about 5 minutes, until golden brown all over • Remove to drain on the kitchen paper

Smoky Aubergine Falafel

Makes 12 falafel

1 aubergine
pinch of salt
pinch of smoked paprika
1 x quantity Falafel Base Mix
    (see page 170)
vegetable oil, for deep frying

Preheat grill to max • Line a baking tray • Large food processor • Large saucepan • Line a tray with kitchen paper

Grill the aubergine • Cut the aubergine into 1cm cubes • Spread over the lined baking tray and sprinkle with the salt and paprika • Grill for 5 minutes, until well softened and starting to blacken ·

Make the aubergine purée • Tip the cooked aubergine into the food processor • Blitz until smooth • Scrape the mixture into a large bowl along with the falafel base mix and stir until well combined

Fry your falafel • Pour the vegetable oil into the saucepan so that it comes no more than two-thirds up the sides of the pan • Set over a high heat • Dip a wooden spoon into the oil and if bubbles form around the spoon, you're ready to cook • Carefully scoop tablespoonfuls of falafel mix into the pan (you may need to do this in batches) • Fry, carefully turning the falafel with a slotted spoon, for about 5 minutes, until golden brown all over • Remove to drain on the kitchen paper

Beetroot Falafel

Makes 12 falafel

80g cooked beetroot
50g chickpeas (drained weight)
2½ tbsp gram flour
5–10g fresh dill
1 quantity Falafel Base Mix
    (see page 170)
vegetable oil, for deep frying

Large food processor • Large saucepan • Line a baking tray with kitchen paper

Make the beetroot purée • Add the beetroot, chickpeas, gram flour and fresh dill, stalks and all, to the food processor • Blitz until smooth • Scrape the mixture into a large bowl along with the falafel base mix and stir until well combined

Fry your falafel • Pour the vegetable oil into the saucepan so that it comes no more than two-thirds up the sides of the pan • Set over a high heat • Dip a wooden spoon into the oil and if bubbles form around the spoon, you're ready to cook • Carefully scoop tablespoonfuls of falafel mix into the pan (you may need to do this in batches) • Fry, carefully turning the falafel with a slotted spoon, for about 5 minutes, until golden brown all over • Remove to drain on the kitchen paper

Best Friends' Dippy Platter

When you have really good friends coming over for drinks and don't want the formality of a sit-down meal, dips are the answer! We've suggested a range of bits for dunking below, but feel free to mix it up with whatever you have to hand: flatbreads, radishes, sugar snaps, fennel or cauliflower would all be glorious. We like to serve our dips chilled, so pop each one into the fridge as you make them, then whip them out when you're ready to serve.

Serves 4

For the Caramelised Onion, Carrot & Cumin Dip
2 onions
2 garlic cloves
1 small carrot
1 tbsp vegetable oil
2 tsp cumin seeds
handful of cashew nuts
2 tbsp egg-free mayo
1 tbsp water
pinch of salt
½ lemon
fennel or dill fronds, to garnish (optional)

For the Red Lentil Hummus
125g red lentils
1 lemon
4 tbsp olive oil, plus extra for drizzling
2 tbsp tahini
1 tsp lazy garlic or 2 garlic cloves, crushed
paprika
salt and black pepper

For the Artichoke & Kale Dip
1 x 280g jar artichokes in oil
100g tinned white beans (cannellini, haricot or butter beans)
30g plant-based parmesan
handful of cashew nuts
pinch of salt
½ lemon
handful of kale leaves

For the crudités
1 red pepper / ½ cucumber / 1 celery stalk / handful of crackers / cherry tomatoes / handful of crisps / a few chicory leaves (optional)

Kettle boiled • Frying pan over a medium heat • Saucepan on a medium-high heat • Food processor • Sieve

Start the Caramelised Onion, Carrot & Cumin Dip • Peel and finely slice the onions and garlic • Peel and grate the carrot • Add the oil to the hot frying pan • Add the onion, carrot, garlic and cumin seeds to the hot oil • Fry for 10 minutes, stirring occasionally

Start the Red Lentil Hummus • Tip the red lentils into the hot saucepan and cover with boiling water • Bring to the boil, reduce the heat and simmer for about 10 minutes, until soft

Make the Artichoke & Kale Dip • Put the artichokes in the food processor with a little oil from the jar • Add the rest of the ingredients, apart from the kale, squeezing in the juice from the lemon half • Blitz until smooth • Pull the kale leaves from their stems, place in a sieve and pour over boiling water • Add the softened leaves to the food processor and pulse a few times until the dip is flecked with green • Add water to loosen, if necessary • Transfer to a bowl and place in the fridge to cool • Rinse out the food processor

Back to the hummus • Drain the lentils and add them to the food processor • Halve the lemon and squeeze in the juice • Add the 4 tablespoons of olive oil, tahini, garlic and salt • Blitz until super smooth and velvety • Add a splash of water to loosen, if necessary • Adjust the seasoning to taste, spoon into a bowl and place in the fridge • Rinse out the food processor

Back to the caramelised onion dip • Put the cashews in the food processor and tip in the well-browned onion and carrot mix • Add the mayo, water and salt • Squeeze in the juice from the lemon half • Blitz to a coarse texture • Spoon into a bowl • Place in the fridge

To serve • Cut the red pepper, cucumber and celery into batons and arrange on a platter along with the crackers, tomatoes, crisps and chicory leaves, if using • Drizzle the hummus with olive oil and sprinkle with paprika • Top the caramelised onion dip with fennel or dill fronds, if you have them

Lighter

04

Roasted Thai Broccoli with Peanut and Coriander Rice Salad

Sometimes, we like to usher an ingredient into the limelight and let it sing. That's what we've done with this recipe. Here, the humble broccoli is getting its chance to shine. The flavours in this dish are rich and zingy, the textures are off-the-chart, but the effort you have to make is minimal. Delicious, packed with flavour and easy to make, this is a winner. And it's great to know that it's also incredibly healthy. Eating the rainbow has never tasted so good.

Serves 4

1 large broccoli head or 400g
    Tenderstem broccoli
3 tbsp vegan Thai green curry paste
1 tbsp sesame oil
2 limes

For the rice salad
1 x 250g pouch pre-cooked rice
2 carrots
¼ red cabbage (about 200g)
50g peanuts
small bunch of fresh coriander
1 fresh red chilli
2–3 spring onions

For the dressing
1 lime
200g coconut yoghurt
2 tbsp peanut butter
salt and black pepper

Preheat grill to high • Line a baking tray • Grater

Start with the broccoli • Cut the broccoli into large florets or leave it whole if using Tenderstem • Put the curry paste in a bowl with the sesame oil and mix them together • Tip in the broccoli and toss well to coat • Spread over the lined baking tray • Halve the limes and add them to the tray • Put under the hot grill until softened and slightly charred at the tips (about 10 minutes for broccoli and 6 minutes for Tenderstem).

Make the rice salad • Heat the rice according to packet instructions and tip it into the bowl used for the broccoli • Peel the carrots, then grate them directly into the bowl • Trim and thinly slice the red cabbage and add it to the bowl • Roughly chop the peanuts and coriander • Slice the red chilli and spring onions • Reserving a handful each of peanuts, coriander, red chilli and spring onion for garnish, add the rest to the mixing bowl and toss well

Make the dressing • Halve the lime and squeeze the juice into a small bowl • Add the coconut yoghurt and peanut butter and mix to combine • Season with salt and black pepper • Toss two thirds of the dressing through the rice salad, reserving the rest

To finish • Remove the tray from the grill and set aside the charred limes • Drizzle the broccoli with the remaining dressing • Top with the reserved coriander, peanuts, red chilli and spring onion • Serve with the rice salad and charred limes

Smashed Cucumber, Watermelon & Sesame Salad

Oh boy, what a salad. Smashing cucumbers (which sounds like a band) allows them to absorb even more of the delicious dressing. They match the watermelon in texture, but contrast in flavour. This salad is a visual feast. Top tip: rinsing the rice noodles in cold water helps to stop them sticking together.

Serves 4

100g rice noodles
1 red onion
1 lime
1 long cucumber
½ small watermelon
3 tbsp sesame seeds
handful of fresh coriander
handful of fresh mint
pinch of chilli flakes
salt

For the dressing
1 lime
2 tbsp soy sauce
1 tbsp olive oil
1 tbsp sesame oil
1 tsp sugar
generous pinch of black pepper

Kettle boiled • Rolling pin • Small frying pan

Start with the noodles • Put the rice noodles in a bowl and cover with boiling water • Leave for 12 minutes

Quickly pickle the onion • Peel and finely slice the red onion and put it in a mixing bowl • Halve one of the limes and squeeze the juice into the bowl • Add a pinch of salt and squeeze the mixture with your hands

Bash the cucumber • Place the cucumber on the chopping board and use a rolling pan to lightly bash it until it splits open • Roughly chop into bite-sized chunks and add to the bowl with the onions • Place the watermelon on the board, cut-side down, and slice into 1cm half moons • Cut off the skin, then cut each slice into 4 wedges • Tip into the bowl with the onions and cucumber • Add a big pinch of salt and toss gently

Make the dressing • Squeeze the juice of the second lime into a bowl • Add the rest of the dressing ingredients and whisk everything together, adding a splash of water to loosen if it's very thick

Toast the sesame seeds • Put a small frying pan over a medium heat • Sprinkle over the sesame seeds and toast until starting to colour • Take off the heat

Finish • Put a plate or your hand over the bowl and carefully tip it over the sink to drain off any liquid that has come out of the salad • Drain the noodles and rinse them with cold water until they are cool • Shake to remove as much water as possible and add the noodles to the salad • Scatter in the toasted sesame seeds • Roughly chop the herbs and add them to the bowl, keeping back a few whole leaves for garnish • Tip the dressing into the bowl and gently toss everything together

Serve • Top the salad with a few whole herb leaves and a pinch of chilli flakes

Green Bean & Sugar Snap Asian Salad

When it comes to salad, a bit of crunch is good. Let's face it, no one wants a soft, soggy salad. This one has really beautiful aromatic flavours, an excellent crunch and – because of the rice – can be served as a main dish. The dressing is creamy and rich and brings the whole dish together beautifully. If you can't find cashew nut butter, don't worry – any creamy nut butter will do.

Serves 4

200g green beans
200g sugar snap peas
1 red chilli
small bunch of fresh coriander
small bunch of fresh mint
1 lime
30g coconut flakes
1 tbsp toasted sesame oil
1 garlic clove
thumb-sized piece of fresh ginger
1 tsp black mustard seeds
2 x 250g pouches pre-cooked
    mixed-grain rice
salt and black pepper

For the nut dressing
1 lime
50ml warm water
3 tbsp cashew butter
    (or any nut butter)
2 tbsp toasted sesame oil
1 tbsp maple syrup
1 tbsp soy sauce
salt and black pepper

Large saucepan of salted water on a high heat • Small frying pan • Large frying pan • Microplane or fine grater

Boil the veg • Bring the pan of salted water to the boil • Add the green beans and sugar snaps to the pan and cook for 3 minutes until bright green • Drain

Make the dressing • Halve the lime and squeeze the juice into a small bowl or jug • Add the rest of the dressing ingredients and whisk together – it may look a little split, but keep whisking until it comes together • Season with salt and pepper

Prepare the garnishes • Finely slice the red chilli • Roughly chop the herbs • Halve the lime • Put a small frying pan over a medium heat • Sprinkle over the coconut flakes and toast until starting to colour • Take off the heat

Fry the greens • Put the large frying pan over a high heat and add the toasted sesame oil • Peel the garlic and grate the garlic and ginger directly into the pan • Add the mustard seeds • Toss and cook for 2 minutes until turning golden • Add the beans and peas and cook for another 2 minutes • Remove from the heat and tip the rice directly into the pan • Toss most of the herbs though, reserving a few for garnish • Season to taste with lime juice and plenty of salt and pepper

Serve • Drizzle the salad with the nut dressing • Top with the reserved herbs, the sliced red chilli and the toasted coconut flakes

Asparagus & Herb Tabbouleh

Regular BOSH! readers will know that we love a mezze spread, and one of the best-known Levantine dishes is tabbouleh. The great thing about tabbouleh is that it's absolutely packed with fresh herbs. Our version combines the usual herby subjects with a generous helping of asparagus, giving it plenty of extra goodness and bite. This dish feels like a salad but fills you up like a main course. And it's packed with goodness, so you can feel good about eating it. A real win all round.

Serves 4–6

250g bulgur wheat
2 large bunches of asparagus
   (500–600g)
50g sunflower seeds
75ml olive oil
2 lemons, or more if needed
1 red onion
1 tbsp ras el hanout
75g pitted dates
small bunch fresh coriander
small bunch fresh mint
small bunch fresh parsley
1 x 400g tin chickpeas
2 tbsp pomegranate seeds
salt and black pepper

For the dressing
150g plant-based yoghurt
2 tbsp tahini
1 tbsp water
salt and black pepper

Large saucepan of salted water on a high heat • Preheat grill to high • Roasting tray

Cook the bulgur wheat • Bring the pan of salted water to the boil • Add the bulgur wheat and cook according to the packet instructions

Grill the asparagus • Trim the asparagus and toss the stems into a roasting tin along with the sunflower seeds • Drizzle over 1 tablespoon of the olive oil and season with salt and pepper • Place under the hot grill to cook for 3–5 minutes, turning occasionally, until softened but still firm

Build the tabbouleh • Slice the lemons in half • Squeeze the juice of 3 halves into a large mixing bowl • Peel and finely chop the red onion and add to the bowl • Add a big pinch of salt and the ras el hanout • Squeeze the onion well with your hands so the lemon juice starts to pickle it • Roughly chop the dates and add them to the bowl • Pick the leaves from the herbs • Reserve a few leaves for garnish and roughly chop the rest • Add the chopped herbs to the bowl

Rinse the bulgur and chickpeas • Tip the cooked bulgur wheat into a colander along with the chickpeas • Rinse with cold water until the bulgur wheat is cool

Make the dressing • Put the dressing ingredients into a bowl and whisk to combine • Squeeze in the juice from the remaining lemon half • Whisk again and season well

Assemble the salad • Tip the drained bulgur wheat and chickpeas into a large dish along with the remaining olive oil • Toss and season with salt and pepper • Taste and add more lemon juice, if needed • Top with the asparagus and sunflower seeds from the roasting tray • Drizzle with the dressing and scatter with the pomegranate seeds and reserved herbs

Salt & Pepper Tofu

Tofu, cooked correctly, is a complete joy. This recipe will show you how to cook tofu to perfection – fluffy on the inside, crunchy on the outside and coated in a wonderfully simple-but-effective selection of peppery spices. A proper restaurant classic.

Serves 4

400g extra-firm tofu
2 tbsp cornflour
1 tbsp salt
1 tbsp ground white pepper
1½ tsp Sichuan peppercorns
3 tbsp vegetable oil

For the noodle salad
300g flat rice noodles
200g Tenderstem broccoli
handful of frozen edamame beans
handful of frozen peas
1½ tbsp tahini
2 tsp soy sauce
2 tsp chilli oil
2 tsp sesame oil
2 limes

To serve
1 fresh green chilli
handful of fresh mint leaves
handful of fresh coriander leaves
2 limes

Kettle boiled • Steamer pan or large saucepan with a colander on a high heat • Frying pan • Line a plate with kitchen paper • Microplane or fine grater

Cook the salad ingredients • Fill the base of the steamer pan or saucepan with boiling water • Add the noodles and cook according to the packet instructions • Place the broccoli, edamame and peas in the upper part of the steamer or colander and set them above the noodles • Cover and steam for 3–4 minutes • Drain the noodles over the veg above the sink, then rinse everything under running cold water and set aside

Prepare the tofu • Cut the tofu into nugget-sized pieces, about 2 x 3cm • Put the cornflour, salt and pepper into a mixing bowl • Bash the Sichuan peppercorns, add them to the cornflour and mix • Add the tofu nuggets, shaking the bowl to coat the tofu and using your hands to gently turn the pieces over in the flour until well covered • Put the frying pan over a medium-high heat and add the vegetable oil • Add the tofu to the hot oil and fry on all sides until crispy • Remove to drain on kitchen paper

Make the noodle salad • Put the tahini, soy sauce and oils in a salad bowl and stir to mix • Zest the limes into the bowl, then halve them and squeeze in the juice • Whisk together to make a dressing, adding a drop of water to loosen, if necessary • Tip in the noodles and veg and toss to coat in the dressing

Serve • Pile a portion of noodle salad onto each plate • Top with the tofu • Finely slice the green chilli and sprinkle it over • Tear over the mint and coriander leaves • Cut the limes into wedges and serve alongside

Broccoli & Mango Miso Salad

Umami – what a word. Here, miso – of which there are many types – adds its uniquely rich and savoury character to a citrussy, peanutty dressing. When drizzled over crunchy broccoli, mango, chilli and herbs, you have a spicy, punchy salad to die for. The star of the show is the sweet, tangy mango, which melts in the mouth and contrasts perfectly with the savoury, sour dressing. Absolutely delightful.

Serves 4 as a side or 2 as a main

400g Tenderstem broccoli
200g frozen peas or edamame beans
1 large mango
small handful of fresh basil leaves
small handful of fresh mint leaves
75g raw peanuts
pinch of chilli flakes (optional)

For the dressing
2 tbsp peanut butter
2 tbsp miso
2 tbsp sriracha
2 tbsp lime juice
1 tbsp water
salt and black pepper

Large saucepan of salted water on a high heat

Cook the vegetables • Finely slice the bottom third of the broccoli stems and put them into a large mixing bowl • Add the tips to the pan of boiling water and cook for 2½ minutes • Add the frozen peas or edamame beans and cook for 30 seconds more • Drain and rinse under very cold running water • Drain and add to the bowl with the broccoli stems

Make the dressing • Add all the ingredients for the dressing to a small bowl and whisk to combine • Season with salt and pepper • Tip the dressing over the vegetables in the bowl

Slice the mango • Prepare the mango by slicing off the 'cheeks' – the flesh on either side of the stone • Cut a cross-hatch pattern into the flesh of each cheek and press on the skin to turn them inside out, popping the cubes outwards • Use a knife or spoon to cut the cubes into the bowl

Finish the salad • Save a few herb leaves for garnish and tear the rest into the bowl • Crumble in most of the peanuts and add the chilli flakes, if using • Toss well • Tip onto a serving platter and garnish with the reserved herbs

Red Pepper Couscous Salad

Couscous is the perfect storecupboard ingredient because it's so effortless and quick to prepare. It makes a great base for a meal, but it's important to pair it with ingredients with different textures. If you like a bit of forward planning, this is definitely a dish you could take to work with you in a lunch box – it tastes as good cold as it does hot.

Serves 4

3 red peppers
1 tbsp olive oil
200g couscous
big pinch of saffron
    or 1 tsp ground turmeric
2 tsp paprika
1 x 400g tin chickpeas
200g cherry tomatoes
70g rocket
130g black olives
75g smoked almonds
large bunch of flat-leaf parsley
salt and black pepper

For the dressing
4 tbsp olive oil
1 tbsp balsamic vinegar
1 tsp sugar
1 lemon
salt and black pepper

Preheat grill to high • Line a baking tray • Kettle boiled

Start with the peppers • Trim the peppers and slice into 2–3cm chunks • Tip onto the lined baking tray • Drizzle with the olive oil and season with salt and pepper • Place under the hot grill for 10 minutes

Start the couscous • Put the couscous, saffron or turmeric and paprika into a bowl • Stir to combine • Pour in enough boiling water to just cover the couscous • Cover and leave for 10 minutes

Make the dressing • Add the oil, vinegar and sugar to a bowl and whisk to combine • Cut the lemon in half and squeeze in the juice of one half • Season with salt and pepper and whisk

Build the salad • Drain and rinse the chickpeas and add them to the mixing bowl • Halve the cherry tomatoes and add them to the bowl along with the rocket and black olives • Roughly chop the smoked almonds and add most of them to the bowl, reserving a few for garnish • Roughly chop the parsley and add it to the bowl

Finish the salad • Use a fork to fluff up the couscous • Squeeze over the juice from the remaining lemon half • Season to taste with salt and pepper • Remove the peppers from the grill • Tip the couscous and red peppers into the mixing bowl with the salad and toss everything together well •

Serve • Tip the salad onto a serving platter and top with the reserved smoked almonds

Taco Salad

Inspired by Mexican tacos (which feature heavily in this book), this salad takes you on a South American flavour journey while packing your body full of plant goodness. We cooked the quinoa and corn cobs for this amazing salad bowl, but you could make it even quicker by using pre-cooked grains and tinned corn. We like to use frozen mango here, as it makes the salad super-refreshing, but fresh mango works great too.

Serves 2

100g uncooked quinoa
    or 250g pre-cooked
1 corn cob or 120g tinned sweetcorn
½ lime
salt

For the black bean, sweetcorn
& mango salad
1 x 400g tin black beans
200g frozen or fresh mango
handful of coriander
1 lime
salt

For the carrot
1 medium carrot
a dash of sesame oil
1 tsp sesame seeds

For the red cabbage
small wedge of red cabbage
½ lime
salt

For the coriander-stalk salsa
handful of fresh coriander stalks
1 tbsp chilli sauce or 1 tsp Tabasco
1 tbsp rapeseed or olive oil
a dash of water
1 lime
salt, to taste

To serve
1 red, yellow or orange pepper,
    or a mix for extra colour
1 avocado
1 fresh red chilli
handful of tortilla chips
handful of fresh coriander leaves
1 lime

Kettle boiled (optional) • Steamer pan or saucepan with a lid and a colander (optional) • Nutribullet or other power blender

Prepare the quinoa and corn • If you're using uncooked quinoa and a fresh corn cob, put the steamer pan or saucepan over a high heat • Add the quinoa and pour over plenty of boiling water • Place the steamer or colander on top • Add the corn cob, cover and cook for 15 minutes • Remove both from the heat, drain the quinoa and cut the corn kernels from the cob, then place both in separate mixing bowls • If using pre-cooked quinoa, heat through according to the packet instructions and place in a mixing bowl • If using tinned corn, simply drain and place in a mixing bowl

Season the quinoa • While the quinoa is still warm, season it well with salt • Squeeze in the juice of the lime half and stir through • Divide between serving bowls and set aside

Prepare the salad • Drain the black beans, add them to the corn and mix lightly • If using fresh mango, trim and cut into chunks • Roughly chop the coriander and halve the lime • Add the mango, coriander, the juice of the lime and a pinch of salt to the blender and pulse until smooth • Add a tablespoon of the mango dressing to the beans and stir through • Transfer the rest of the dressing to a small bowl • Rinse out the blender

Prep the rest of the veg and the salsa • Peel and grate the carrot into a bowl • Add the sesame oil and seeds and mix • Shred the cabbage, put it in a bowl and dress it with the juice of the lime half and some salt • Add all the salsa ingredients, including the zest and juice of the lime, to the blender • Blitz until smooth • Deseed and slice the peppers and avocado • Finely slice the red chilli

Assemble the bowls • Working in a circle on top of the quinoa base, pile each salad element into the bowls, finishing with handfuls of tortilla chips, spoonfuls of the reserved mango dressing and a dollop of the coriander-stalk salsa in the middle of each bowl • Top with the chopped chilli and some coriander leaves • Cut the lime into wedges and serve alongside

Chimichurri Couscous

If you're into punchy flavours, this dish is for you – it's a true taste explosion. There's tanginess, smokiness, spiciness, freshness, saltiness, zingyness. You name it, when it comes to flavour, this dish has got it. This will go down a treat at dinnertime, but will also be lovely the next day for lunch.

Serves 4

120g couscous

For the roast veg
2 courgettes
2 red onions
2 garlic cloves
2 tbsp olive oil
½ lemon
3 jarred red peppers
salt

For the chimichurri
handful of fresh coriander
handful of fresh parsley
½ fresh red chilli
1 tbsp capers
4 tbsp extra-virgin olive oil
1 tsp red wine vinegar
salt

For the tofu
1 tbsp olive oil
150g smoked tofu

Preheat oven to 250°C • Kettle boiled • Large roasting tray • Small food processor • Frying pan

Make the couscous • Put the couscous in a large bowl • Pour over enough boiling water to just cover the grains • Cover and set aside

Make the roast veg • Halve the courgettes lengthways, then slice quite thinly • Peel the onions and cut each into 8 wedges • Put the veg into a roasting tray along with the whole, unpeeled garlic cloves, olive oil and a generous sprinkling of salt • Squeeze over the juice of the lemon and chuck the squeezed half into the tray, too • Roast on the top shelf of the oven for 15 minutes, until soft and slightly browned • Slice the jarred peppers and set them aside for later

Make the chimichurri • Reserve a few herb leaves for garnish and place the rest of the herbs, stalk and all, in the food processor along with all the other chimichurri ingredients • Whizz until fairly smooth • Carefully remove the garlic cloves from the roasting tray and squeeze the flesh into the food processor • Pulse a few more times to combine

Cook the tofu • Put the frying pan over a medium-high heat and add the olive oil • Slice the tofu into 3cm strips • Add to the hot oil and fry until golden all over

To serve • Fluff up the couscous grains with a fork • Add half the chimichurri to the couscous and mix • Add the roasted veg • Squeeze over any remaining juice from the roasted lemon and discard • Add the sliced jarred peppers • Mix very lightly to keep the couscous bouncy, then divide between 4 bowls • Drizzle over the remaining chimichurri • Lay the sliced tofu on top • Sprinkle over the reserved herbs to garnish

Teriyaki Tempeh

If we don't get to eat this every month, we throw a tempeh tantrum! Seriously though, tempeh is an absolutely delicious source of protein, with a rich, meaty texture and the ability to take on flavour once you've blanched it. We like to hit ours with sweet, sticky sauce and combine with a speedy sesame rice and, as always, get some greens in, too.

Serves 2

200g tempeh
1 tbsp vegetable oil
large handful of cashew nuts

For the teriyaki sauce
4 tbsp soy sauce
2 tbsp maple syrup
1 tbsp light brown sugar
1 tsp Chinese vinegar
    or rice wine vinegar
¼ tsp ginger paste or a few
    gratings of fresh ginger
¼ tsp lazy garlic or 1 grated clove
2 tsp cornflour
1 tbsp water

For the sesame rice & greens
80g basmati rice
large handful of green beans
    or Tenderstem broccoli
    or kale, or a mix
1 tbsp sesame oil
generous pinch of salt

To serve
1 spring onion
3cm piece fresh ginger
1 tbsp sesame seeds
    (optional)

Kettle boiled • Saucepan with a lid or a steamer pan • Small saucepan on a low heat • Frying pan • Microplane or fine grater

Prepare the tempeh • Fill the saucepan with boiling water, add the tempeh and blanch for 5 minutes (or steam it in a steamer)

Meanwhile, make the teriyaki sauce • Put the soy sauce, maple syrup, sugar, vinegar, ginger and garlic into the small saucepan and stir until the sugar has dissolved • Put the cornflour into a small bowl with the water and mix to make a slurry • Add to the pan and stir until slightly thickened and glossy • Remove from the heat

Marinate the tempeh • Drain the tempeh and cut it into strips • Tip it into the pan with the teriyaki sauce and toss to coat • Set aside • Rinse the pan and boil the kettle again

Boil the rice • Put the rice in the saucepan, cover generously with boiling water and bring to the boil • Reduce the heat to low and simmer for 10 minutes

Meanwhile, cook the tempeh • Put the frying pan over a medium heat and add the vegetable oil • Add the tempeh to the hot oil, reserving any teriyaki sauce that gets left behind • Fry for 6–8 minutes, until dark brown all over, adding the cashews to the pan after 3 minutes to cook alongside the tempeh

Back to the rice • After 10 minutes of simmering, the rice will be pretty much done, so chuck in your greens, cover and cook for 3 minutes • Drain, drizzle over the sesame oil and sprinkle with the salt, then cover loosely with a clean tea towel until ready to serve

Serve • Divide the sesame rice and greens between 2 plates and top with the tempeh • Brush over any teriyaki sauce you have left • Slice the spring onion and scatter it over the top • Grate over some ginger and scatter over the sesame seeds, if using

Winter Roots Salad

In winter, salads can sometimes get overlooked in favour of warmer, cosier dishes. But roasted root veg can be used in salads, too! Here speedily roasted baby carrots and parsnips, toasted garlic bread and sweet little cranberries are tossed in a light, creamy dressing. Lovely to eat on a fresh winter's day.

Serves 2

150g baby carrots
150g baby parsnips
3–4 tbsp olive oil
3 garlic cloves
1 medium baguette (about 150g)
2 red onions
2 tsp cumin seeds
2 tsp caraway seeds
100g kale
1 lemon
large handful of fresh mint leaves
bunch of flat-leaf parsley
2 tbsp dried cranberries or raisins
salt and black pepper

For the dressing

½ lemon
3 tbsp dairy-free crème fraîche
1 tsp Dijon mustard
1 tsp maple syrup
salt and black pepper

Preheat oven to 220°C • Large saucepan of salted water on a high heat • 2 large roasting tins • Colander • Kettle boiled

Start with the root veg • Peel and chop the carrots and parsnips into batons, if necessary • Add to the pan of boiling water and boil for 5 minutes

Prepare the croutons • Pour 2 tablespoons of the olive oil into one of the roasting tins • Peel the garlic cloves, crush with the back of a knife and add them to the tin, mixing them with the oil as you do so • Tear the baguette into croutons and toss them straight into the tin • Coat the bread with the garlic oil • Season with a big pinch of salt and pepper • Slide the tin onto the middle shelf of the oven and roast for 15–20 minutes, until crisp

Return to the veg • Drain the carrots and parsnips and tip them into the second roasting tin • Peel the red onions, cut them into wedges and add them to the tray • Drizzle with 1 tablespoon of olive oil and scatter with the cumin and caraway seeds • Put the roasting tin on the top shelf of the oven and roast for 20 minutes

Prepare the kale • Tip the kale into a colander and pour over boiling water to shock and soften it slightly • Drain then tip into a large bowl • Halve the lemon and squeeze over the juice • Massage the kale with your hands for 2–3 minutes, until softened • Pick the leaves from the herbs and roughly chop them

Make the dressing • Squeeze the lemon juice into a small bowl • Add the rest of the dressing ingredients and whisk to combine • Season to taste

Make the salad • Remove both tins from the oven • Tip the croutons into the tin with the roasted vegetables • Toss well • Add the herbs, kale and cranberries or raisins and toss again • Drizzle generously with the dressing and serve warm

Turmeric-Roasted Cauli Wedges

If our mums told us we were having cauliflower for tea when we were kids, we'd roll our eyes and moan. How things have changed! Cauliflower is now one of our favourite vegetables because of creative, delicious recipes just like this. This dish has a wonderful blend of spices, sweetness and texture and it's super-duper healthy. If you're a fan of cauliflower, you need to give this a try. Deeelicious. This is lovely served with lemon yoghurt or mango chutney.

Serves 4 (with leftovers)

2 tsp ground turmeric
3 tbsp olive oil
1 large cauliflower
salt and black pepper

For the rice & lentil salad
2 x 250g pouches pre-cooked
    brown rice
1 x 250g pouch pre-cooked Puy lentils
small bunch of fresh mint
small bunch of flat-leaf parsley
150g dried apricots
2 lemons
2 tsp cumin seeds
2 tsp coriander seeds
3 tbsp olive oil
salt and black pepper

To serve
coconut flakes

Preheat oven to 220°C • Line a baking tray • Frying pan • Pestle and mortar

Heat the rice and lentils • Heat the rice and lentils according to the packet instructions • Tip into a bowl and mix together

Prepare the cauliflower • Add the turmeric and olive oil to a large mixing bowl along with a generous grinding of salt and pepper • Trim the cauliflower and remove any old leaves • Toss some of the younger leaves into the bowl • Chop the rest of the cauliflower into wedges and add them to the bowl • Toss in the turmeric oil • Tip onto the baking tray and bake in the hot oven for 15 minutes

Return to the salad • Reserving a few leaves for garnish, roughly chop the herbs and apricots • Add them to the bowl with the rice and lentils • Halve the lemons and squeeze in the juice

Toast the coconut and spices • Put the frying pan over a high heat • Add the coconut flakes and toast until lightly browned • Tip into a bowl and set aside, returning the pan to the heat • Add the cumin and coriander seeds to the pan and toast for around 1 minute, until really fragrant • Transfer to a pestle and mortar and crush • Add the spices to the rice and lentil bowl along with the olive oil • Toss to combine • Taste and season with salt and black pepper

Serve • Arrange the salad on a serving platter • Scatter over the roasted cauliflower • Top with the toasted coconut flakes and the reserved herbs

Crispy Baby Corn Salad

Baby corn never seems to take centre stage, so we decided to write a recipe that gives it the attention it deserves. This salad is crunchy, fresh and delicious – perfect for a light lunch on a sunny summer's day. The dressing combines the kick of mustard, the zip of lemon and the 'mmm' of sweet chilli sauce to create a well-rounded, incredibly moreish salad.

Serves 4

1 tbsp olive oil, plus extra for drizzling
1 tsp smoked paprika
175g baby corn
1 red onion
2 limes
2 x 400g tins black beans
200g cherry tomatoes
2 baby gem lettuce
2 ripe avocados
2 tbsp sliced jalapeños from a jar
small bunch of fresh coriander leaves
30g shop-bought roasted
    and salted corn
salt and black pepper

For the dressing
2 limes
3 tbsp olive oil
2 tsp sweet chilli sauce
1 tsp Dijon mustard

Preheat grill to high • Line a baking tray

Grill the corn • Add the tablespoon of olive oil and the paprika to a large mixing bowl and mix to combine • Chop the baby corn into thirds and add to the bowl • Season with salt and tip onto the baking tray • Grill for 8–10 minutes, until the corn is a little charred • Keep the bowl for the dressing

Pickle the red onion • Peel and finely slice the red onion • Tip into a bowl • Halve the limes and squeeze in the juice • Use your hands to massage the onion a bit • Season with salt and set aside

Make the dressing • Halve the limes and squeeze the juice into the bowl used for the baby corn • Add the rest of the dressing ingredients and whisk to combine

Build your salad • Drain and rinse the black beans • Halve the cherry tomatoes • Separate the baby gem leaves • Peel and stone the avocado and cut it into wedges • Add the beans, tomatoes, lettuce leaves and avocado to the bowl along with the jalapeños and the pickled onions

To finish • Once the corn is cooked, remove it from the grill and let it cool for a couple of minutes before adding it to the bowl • Roughly chop and add the coriander • Gently toss everything together • Slide onto a serving platter • Drizzle with a little extra olive oil, scatter with the crunchy roasted corn and finish with a crack of black pepper

Sweet

05

Banana Microwave Cake

Need a showstopping dessert or birthday cake in a hurry? We've got you covered! The sponge for this cake is cooked in the microwave so it really is the work of moments. The key here is not to hold back on the decoration – we heartily approve of throwing the contents of your baking cupboard at this one. It's definitely a case of more-is-more so let your inner (or actual) kid go to town.

Serves 8

75ml vegetable oil, plus
    extra for greasing
125ml unsweetened plant-based milk
1 tsp vanilla extract
4 tbsp milled flaxseeds
2 bananas
100g caster sugar
175g plain flour
2 tsp baking powder
½ tsp salt

For the icing
50g peanut butter
75g plant-based butter
50g icing sugar

To decorate
fresh or maraschino cherries
banana chips
dairy-free chocolate sauce
dairy-free squirty cream (optional)
coloured vegan-friendly
    sprinkles (optional)

Pasta bowl or baking dish that will fit in your microwave (ours was about 15cm at the base and 21cm at the rim) • Baking paper (optional) • Food processor • Microwave

Prep your baking dish • Grease the baking dish and line it with baking paper if you plan to take the cake out of the dish before serving, letting the paper overhang the edges slightly (if you're serving it in the dish you don't need to line it)

Make the cake batter • Put the oil, plant-based milk, vanilla extract and milled flaxseeds into the food processor and blend until smooth • Peel and chop the bananas and add them to the processor, then pulse until smooth • Put the sugar, flour, baking powder and salt into a bowl and mix to combine • Add the mixture to the processor and pulse just until you have a smooth batter – be careful not to overmix

Cook the cake • Pour the batter into the dish and spread it out to an even layer • Microwave for 8 minutes at 800W • Let the cake stand for 2 minutes, then lift out of the plate with the baking paper (or leave it in the dish) • Let it cool completely, then keep it in the fridge until you're ready to decorate it

Make the icing • Put the peanut butter, plant-based butter and golden icing sugar in the food processor and blend until pale and creamy

Decorate • Remove the baking paper, if necessary • Spread the icing over the top of the cake • Decorate with cherries, banana chips, chocolate sauce, dairy-free squirty cream and vegan-friendly sprinkles, if using, just before serving

Cronuts

Croissants + donuts = cronuts! Invented by master baker Dominique Ansel, the cronut combines the crispy flakiness of croissant dough with the gorgeous, naughty, deep-fried appeal of a donut. Well, guess what... ours take less than 30 minutes! We've hacked the dough by double folding a puff pastry sheet, so you can enjoy these beauties in a fraction of the usual time. Remember to work quickly so the pastry stays as firm as possible.

Makes 12

40g plant-based butter
40g caster sugar, plus
    extra for sprinkling
1 heaped tsp (10g) baking powder
1 x 320g sheet ready-rolled
    dairy-free puff pastry
vegetable oil, for deep-frying

To serve
120g jam (optional)

Rolling pin • Large heavy-based saucepan • Line a tray with kitchen paper

First make the sugar mixture • Put the butter, sugar and baking powder in a bowl and mix together until smooth and well combined

Roll the pastry • Unroll the pastry on its baking paper with the long edge nearest you • Use a rolling pin to quickly roll the pastry out to the same size as its paper • Mentally split your pastry sheet into thirds and spread a third of the sugar mixture over the middle strip, leaving a 3cm gap at the edges • Fold the right side of the pastry over to seal the middle third • Pat the top gently with your fingers to slightly flatten it all over • Spread another third of the sugar mixture over the top, again leaving a 3cm gap at the edges • Fold the left side of the pastry over and gently pat with your fingers • Spread the remaining sugar mixture over the top, again leaving a 3cm gap top and bottom • Carefully pick up the bottom edge of the pastry (nearest you) and roll up the pastry into a sausage shape, using the baking paper to help roll it • Pinch along the seam of the pastry to seal it as much as possible • Once rolled, twist the ends of the paper like a Christmas cracker • Place in the freezer for 10 minutes to firm up

Prepare the oil for deep frying • Pour enough oil into the saucepan until it comes no more than two-thirds up the side of the pan • Heat the oil to 180°C, or until a wooden spoon dipped into the oil sizzles around the edges

Cut the cronuts • Remove the pastry from the freezer and unwrap it • Use your fingers to press down along the join, ensuring it's well sealed • Use a very sharp knife to quickly cut the pastry into 8 equal-sized discs

Fry the cronuts • Carefully lower each cronut into the hot oil and fry in batches until golden and puffed up, around 3-4 minutes on each side, gently turning them in the pan to cook evenly • Remove to drain on kitchen paper • Sprinkle with extra sugar while they are still hot • Serve with a dollop of jam in the middle of each cronut, if you like

Fruit & Nut Cornflake Cakes

There's something about these simple pantry treats that's reminiscent of being at your nan's house as a kid. They're sweet and nostalgic, like all the best treats are. We've ramped up the nostalgia even further and given them a BOSH! twist by lacing them with the flavours of one of our favourite chocolate bars growing up. We challenge you not to lick the bowl!

Makes 12

300g dark chocolate
100g mixed nuts
75g plant-based butter
90g golden syrup
60g cornflakes
60g Rice Krispies
125g flame raisins
2 ginger or speculoos
    biscuits (optional)

Line a 12-hole muffin tin with muffin cases • Microwaveable bowl or small saucepan and heatproof bowl • Microwave (optional) • Food processor or blender • Large ice-cream scoop

Melt the chocolate • Roughly chop the chocolate and place it in the microwaveable bowl • Either melt it in the microwave in 30-second blasts or pour hot water into the bottom of a saucepan and bring to a simmer, put the bowl on top of the pan and leave the chocolate to melt • Once melted, mix until smooth

Make the cake mix • Roughly chop the nuts • Place the butter, golden syrup and a quarter of the melted chocolate into the food processor • Blend for about 1 minute, until fluffy and light • Gradually add the rest of the melted chocolate and pulse until smooth • Scrape the mixture into a large bowl • Add the cornflakes, Rice Krispies, chopped nuts and raisins • Fold together so that everything is evenly coated in the chocolate mixture

Shape and finish • Use the ice-cream scoop to add generous mounds of the mixture to the cupcake cases and press down to help compact them • Crumble the ginger or speculoos biscuits, if using, over the tops of the cakes • Transfer to the fridge to chill for 15 minutes

Rice Krispie Donuts

This kind of donut is super-easy to make and doesn't need frying, which is always a bonus! We use good old-fashioned Rice Krispies mixed with melted chocolate and golden syrup to get it super sticky so that the donuts set. There are loads of ways you can jazz these up, so why not make a few of each? They make the perfect party treats for kids (or kids at heart!). We've shown you how to make three different toppings: chocolate, vanilla and Biscoff, and we recommend you make all three to add variety to your donut spread.

Makes 12

250g dark chocolate
1 tbsp smooth peanut butter
100g Rice Krispies
75g golden syrup
1 tbsp shop-bought squeezy
    vegan chocolate sauce

For the quick vanilla frosting
50g icing sugar
½ tbsp unsweetened plant-based milk
½ tsp vanilla extract

For the quick biscuit frosting
2 tbsp unsweetened plant-based milk
1½ tbsp Biscoff spread

For the toppings (optional)
30g dark chocolate
30g vegan-friendly hundreds
    and thousands

Silicone donut moulds (12 cups) • Large microwaveable bowl • Microwave • Whisk • Set a wire rack over a sheet of baking paper

Make the donuts • Put the chocolate and peanut butter in a large microwaveable bowl and microwave for 30 seconds • Stir and repeat until the chocolate has melted • Stir again, then add the Rice Krispies and golden syrup and fold in • Spoon the mixture into the donut moulds and put them in the freezer to set

Make the quick vanilla frosting • Put all the ingredients in a bowl and whisk until smooth

Make the quick biscuit frosting • Put all the ingredients in a bowl and whisk until smooth

Assemble the donuts • If you're topping with dark chocolate, chop it finely and set it aside • Remove the donut trays from the freezer and turn the donuts out onto the wire rack • Drizzle 4 of the donuts with vegan chocolate sauce • Dip the whisk into the vanilla frosting and wave it over 4 of the donuts in a zig-zag pattern • Wipe the whisk clean and repeat to drizzle the remaining 4 donuts with the biscuit frosting • Sprinkle over the optional toppings

Spice Dust Chocolate Truffles

Fancy feeling like a proper chocolatier, but without spending all your Sunday afternoons in the kitchen? We've got you covered. In chocolate. These truffles can be whipped up in a jiffy, and we've used a couple of secret ingredients: kidney beans for chewy, creamy, smoothness (weird – but, trust us, it works) and crushed Oreos to help them set. BOSH!

Makes about 34

300g dark chocolate
125g plant-based butter
150g golden caster sugar
60g Oreos
1 tsp vanilla extract
10g cocoa powder
1 x 210g tin kidney beans
  (130g drained weight)
100g raisins

For the spice dust
100g hazelnuts
heaped ½ tsp ground cinnamon
½ tsp ground ginger
4½ tbsp Demerara sugar

Microwaveable bowl or small saucepan and a heatproof bowl • Frying pan • Food processor • Wide shallow bowl or line a baking tray with baking paper

Melt the chocolate • Roughly chop the chocolate and place it in the microwaveable bowl • Either melt it in the microwave in 30-second blasts or pour hot water into the bottom of a saucepan and bring to a simmer, put the bowl on top of the pan and leave the chocolate to melt • Once melted, mix until smooth

Roast the hazelnuts • Put a frying pan over a medium–high heat • Add the hazelnuts and roast until golden • Take off the heat and set aside to cool

Make the truffle mixture • Put the butter and sugar into a food processor and blend for 2 minutes until pale and creamy • Roughly break up the Oreos and add them to the processor along with the vanilla and cocoa powder • Drain and rinse the kidney beans and add them to the processor • Blend until smooth and creamy • Add the melted chocolate and pulse until combined • Stir in the raisins • Spread the mixture in an even layer in the shallow bowl or a lined baking tray and place in the freezer for 5 minutes to firm up

Make the spice dust • Finely chop the hazelnuts and put them in a bowl with the spices and sugar • Mix well

Finish • Take the truffle mixture out of the freezer • Roll heaped teaspoons of the mixture into balls between your palms • Roll in the spice dust to coat

Ice Cream Tiramisu

Desserts don't come much more decadent than this. Ice cream, coffee, chocolate, alcohol and croissant – ALL AT THE SAME TIME! It's obviously gonna be good. If you're hosting a dinner party, make it. If it's date night, make it. If your parents are visiting, make it. If you've passed an exam, make it. If you've survived another day, make it. You really don't need much more of an excuse than that. This can be made ahead and stored in the freezer – freezing squirty cream may seem a bit strange but, trust us, it works!

Serves 4–6

4 dairy-free croissants
80ml Marsala, dessert wine or brandy
80ml hot, strong coffee
20g light muscovado or soft
   light brown sugar

For the topping
400ml dairy-free vanilla, coffee
   or chocolate ice cream
½ x can dairy-free squirty cream
1 tbsp cocoa powder
5–10g dark chocolate

20–24cm serving dish • Preheat grill to high • Make the hot, strong coffee • Ice cream scoop • Sieve • Microplane or fine grater

Make the base • Slice the dairy-free croissants in half lengthways • Toast under the hot grill until just golden, about 1 minute • Place in the serving dish • Put the Marsala, coffee and sugar in a bowl and mix together • Pour the mixture over the croissants, pressing lightly to help the liquid soak in • Leave for 10 minutes • Take the ice cream out of the freezer to soften

Assemble • Scoop the slightly softened ice cream over the soaked croissants, spreading it out to make a fairly even layer • Squirt the cream over the top in pretty swirls • Sift over the cocoa powder, then finish with a grating of chocolate • Serve immediately or store in the freezer until required, removing to thaw slightly 10 minutes before you want to serve

Coffee Caramel Tearer Sharer

If you're a coffee cake lover, but keen not to spend hours in the kitchen, then this is for you! A super-easy dessert that's filled with all that toasty brown sugar and coffee flavour, but with the oh-so-satisfying flaky crumble of puff pastry. The flavours coming out of this dish are to die for – you're gonna love it. We promise.

Serves 8

50g plant-based butter
    at room temperature
50g light muscovado sugar
¾ tsp ground cinnamon
1 tsp vanilla extract
    or vanilla bean paste
1 heaped tsp espresso powder
1 x 320g ready-rolled dairy-free
    puff pastry sheet
80g Biscoff spread
100g pecans

To decorate and serve
dark chocolate (optional)
dairy-free vanilla ice cream
espressos

Preheat oven to 200°C • Microwaveable bowl • Baking sheet

Make the coffee spread • Put the plant-based butter, sugar, cinnamon, vanilla and espresso powder in the microwavable bowl and mix until smooth • Set aside

Fill the pastry • Unroll the pastry on its sheet of baking paper and position it horizontally so the wide edge is nearest you • Spread the bottom half of the pastry with the Biscoff spread • Spread the top half with a heaped tablespoon of the coffee spread • Roughly chop the pecans and scatter two-thirds all over the surface of the pastry, reserving the rest • Fold the top half of the pastry down to meet the bottom half and seal in the filling • Roughly pat down

Shape the pastry • Find the centre of the closest edge to you and cut vertically, stopping 2cm from the furthest edge • Make 3 more even slices either side so that you have 7 slices and 8 pastry 'arms' joined together at the far edge • Carefully lift the two end pieces and form the pastry into a snowflake shape (see photo, *right*), letting the pastry overlap at the folded edge • Lift the pastry on its baking paper onto the baking sheet • Twist each pastry 'arm' evenly about 4 times

Bake • Put the baking sheet on the middle shelf of the hot oven and bake for 15–20 minutes, until cooked through and golden • Remove from the oven and leave to cool for 5 minutes

Serve • Meanwhile, heat the remaining coffee spread in the microwave for about 30 seconds to make a sauce • Chop the chocolate, if using • Either serve the pastry straight from the tray or lift it onto a board on its paper • Sprinkle over the remaining chopped pecans and the chopped chocolate, if using • Drizzle over the coffee sauce • Serve with ice cream and espressos

Spectaculoos Cupcakes

If you visit a coffee shop in mainland Europe, there's a high chance that the waiter will give you a little speculoos biscuit with your espresso. We love the flavour of those little biscuits, so we made these delicious cupcakes using Biscoff spread to achieve the wonderful, caramel-like continental flavour that goes so well with coffee. If you're a fan of proper coffee and you fancy a little treat, make a batch of these spectaculoos cupcakes – you won't be disappointed.

Makes 12

160g self-raising flour
110g caster sugar
60g butter
60g Biscoff spread
1 tsp bicarbonate of soda
75ml unsweetened unsweetened
    plant-based milk
1 tsp cider vinegar
1 tsp vanilla extract

For the icing
100g plant-based butter straight
    from the fridge
80g Biscoff spread
50g icing sugar
1 tsp vanilla extract

To decorate
50g pecans or hazelnuts
60g dark chocolate
12 cherries

Preheat the oven to 180°C • Line a 12-hole cupcake tin with paper cases • Frying pan • Electric hand-held beaters

Make the cupcakes • Put all the cupcake ingredients in a large mixing bowl and use electric beaters to beat until smooth • Divide equally between the cupcake cases • Bake in the oven for 12–15 minutes, until golden and cooked through • Leave to cool in the tin • Clean and dry the bowl

Meanwhile, toast the nuts • Put a frying pan over a medium-high heat • Add the nuts and toast until golden • Take off the heat and set aside to cool, then chop • Roughly chop the chocolate

Make the icing • Put all the icing ingredients in the clean bowl and use electric beaters to beat until smooth and creamy • Keep in the fridge until the cupcakes are cool

Decorate • Spread the icing over the cooled cupcakes • Top with cherries, then sprinkle over the toasted nuts and chocolate

D's Gooey Choconut Ganache

Chocolatey goodness mixed with candied nuts and creamy coconut create an absolute winner of a dessert here. Our housemate Darren (aka Bodyweight D, aka D) loves this dessert so much that we had to name it after him! It's a gooey ganache and must be kept in the fridge, but it's deliciously sweet and incredibly indulgent. It goes great on its own or served with a spoonful of dairy-free ice cream.

Makes 24 squares or 12 bars

300g dark chocolate
100ml coconut milk
100g caster sugar
1 tsp vanilla extract
100g almond butter

For the salted caramel hazelnuts
100g caster sugar
150g blanched hazelnuts
1 tsp sea salt, plus extra
   for sprinkling

Grease and line a 28 x 22cm traybake tin with baking paper • Line a baking tray with baking paper • Large heavy-based frying pan • Small heavy-based saucepan

Make the salted caramel hazelnuts • Put the sugar and nuts into the frying pan and set it over a medium heat • Cook, stirring regularly, for 5–8 minutes, until the sugar has melted and caramelised, keeping a close eye on it • Once melted and golden, stir in the teaspoon of salt • Spread the mixture over the lined baking tray in an even layer • Leave to cool for 5 minutes

Make the ganache • Finely chop the chocolate • Put the coconut milk, sugar and vanilla into the small saucepan and place it over a medium heat • Stir until melted and smooth, but don't let it boil • Remove from the heat, then add the chocolate • Leave it for 1–2 minutes so the chocolate can melt, then fold together until smooth

Assemble • Break up the caramelised hazelnuts, then sprinkle half into the traybake tin • Pour the chocolate mixture over the top • Add dollops of the almond butter and loosely swirl it through the mixture using the tip of a knife • Sprinkle over the rest of the nuts and an extra sprinkling of sea salt, if you like • Leave to cool then transfer to the fridge to set for 1 hour before slicing into squares or bars

Creamy Lime Pie

When we were last in America, we ate a whole bunch of lemon and lime pies – they love that stuff out there! As it happens, so do we, so we were super keen to find a way to make a version that would transport us right back to the US of A in a fraction of the time that it would usually take to rustle up this awesome dessert. And we did it! Although the cooking is done in 30 minutes, it does need to set in the fridge for about 3 hours, so it's a great dessert to make ahead when you've got people coming over for dinner. There will be no leftovers!

Serves 8

120g plant-based butter
300g digestive biscuits
60g demerara or granulated sugar

For the filling
4 limes
300g silken tofu
3 tsp vanilla extract
100g plant-based butter
300g icing sugar
20g cornflour

For the topping
dairy-free squirty cream

Preheat oven to 180°C • Grease a deep 23cm pie dish • Microwaveable bowl • Microwave • Food processor • Microplane or fine grater • Small saucepan

Make the biscuit base • Put the butter in the microwavable bowl and microwave on full power for 30 seconds • Put the biscuits in the food processor and whizz until crushed • Add the melted butter and sugar and whizz until well combined • Tip the mixture into the pie dish and press it into the base and sides to make an even crust about 8mm thick • Bake in the hot oven for 10 minutes • Clean out the bowl of the food processor

Make the filling • Zest and juice the limes • Drain the tofu, then add to the food processor along with the vanilla, plant-based butter, icing sugar, cornflour and half the lime zest and juice • Blend until smooth • Scrape the mixture into the small saucepan and bring to the boil over a high heat • Reduce to a medium simmer and cook for 10 minutes, mixing regularly, until thick and creamy

Assemble the pie • Beat the rest of the lime zest and juice into the filling mixture then pour into the biscuit base • Set aside to cool for about 40 minutes, then transfer to the fridge to set for at least 3 hours, or ideally overnight

Serve • Cut into slices and top with swirls of dairy-free squirty cream

Millionaire's Shortbread

Walking home from school was always fun; chatting to mates, kicking a ball about and, best of all, spending leftover lunch money at the local bakery. We were both very fond of their millionaire's shortbread, so we decided to make our own. These beauties have everything – rich chocolate, gooey caramel and a crunchy biscuit base. Make a batch next time your mum's coming round for a cuppa: brownie points guaranteed. We're very proud that we've managed to turn these wonderful bites into a speedy recipe. Enjoy!

Makes 16

200g plain flour
100g plant-based butter
pinch of salt
50g caster sugar
200g dark chocolate

For the caramel
300g pitted dates
40ml boiling water
75g plant-based butter
100g light muscovado sugar
150ml golden or maple syrup
2 tsp vanilla extract
   or vanilla bean paste
100g Biscoff spread

Preheat oven to 180ºC • Grease and line a 20 x 30cm baking tin with baking paper • Food processor • Microwaveable bowl and microwave or saucepan and a heatproof bowl

Make the biscuit base • Measure the flour, plant-based butter, salt and sugar into a mixing bowl • Rub with your fingertips until the mixture looks like crumble • Tip into the prepared tin and lightly press down with your fingers until even • Bake on the middle shelf of the oven for 12 minutes • Remove and set aside to cool in the tin

Meanwhile, make the caramel • Put the dates and boiling water in a food processor • Blend until smooth • Add the plant-based butter, sugar, syrup, vanilla and Biscoff spread and blend until smooth and thick

Melt the chocolate • Roughly chop the chocolate and place it in the microwaveable bowl • Either melt it in the microwave in 30-second blasts or pour hot water into the bottom of a saucepan and bring to a simmer, put the bowl on top of the pan and leave the chocolate to melt • Once melted, mix until smooth

Assemble • Dollop the caramel over the biscuit base and gently spread it out to an even layer • Pour over an even layer of the melted chocolate • Leave to cool, then transfer to the fridge to set for 2 hours • Heat a sharp knife under the hot tap and use it to slice the shortbread into squares

Portuguese Custard Tarts

These lovely little tarts, also known as *pastel de nata*, were originally created by Portuguese monks. It's hard to believe they'll work when you're making them, but the speedy shop-bought puff pastry comes together perfectly to form a base. Our silken tofu and Biscoff filling is absolutely incredible, and topped off with a touch of cinnamon, this is a truly delicious pastry. We've come up with a lot of recipes that make people say 'there's no way that's vegan', and these Portuguese custard tarts are one of them.

Makes 12

1 x 320g sheet dairy-free puff pastry
20g caster sugar
ground cinnamon
plant-based butter, for greasing

For the filling
1 small lemon
1 x 300g pack silken tofu
190g icing sugar
40g Biscoff spread
20g cornflour
4 tsp vanilla bean paste
15g tahini
160ml oat cream

Preheat oven to 220°C • Grease the holes and outer rims of a 12-hole muffin tin • Microplane or fine grater • Food processor • Small saucepan • Whisk

Prepare the pastry cases • Working quickly, unroll the pastry sheet and cut it in half lengthways • Cut each long strip widthways to make 6 rectangles • Use the pastry to line the holes of the muffin tin, pressing and nipping to fit roughly and come up over the edges of each hole – don't worry about being neat • Sprinkle the caster sugar over the pastry • Bake on the top shelf of the oven for 10 minutes • Remove the tin and quickly press the middle of each tart down with the handle of a wooden spoon • Return to the oven to bake for another 5 minutes

Make the filling • Zest and juice the lemon – you want about 1 tablespoon of juice – and set it aside • Drain the tofu • Put all the filling ingredients, except the lemon zest and juice, into the food processor and blitz until smooth • Set the saucepan over a medium heat • Pour the mixture into the pan and simmer gently for 5–7 minutes, whisking all the time, until it forms a thick, wobbly custard • Whisk in the lemon zest and juice

Fill the pastry cases • Divide the filling between the pastry cases • Sprinkle each tart with a little ground cinnamon • Leave to firm up for 20 minutes before eating, but loosen in the tin before they cool completely so they don't stick

Rocky BOSH! Bars

Baking is fun, but we're all busy, right? This rocky road is fast, no-bake and, of course, absolutely delicious. Pretzels, Rice Krispies and Oreos (yes, we went there) combine with the best dark chocolate you can find to create a chocolatey delight that's ready in minutes. Beware as this is super moreish - it might be worth popping some in Tupperware for your neighbours so that you don't eat them all...

Makes 16 small bars

400g dark chocolate
150g golden or maple syrup
150g plant-based butter
100g salted pretzels
250g Oreos
80g ginger nuts (or other biscuits)
100g Rice Krispies

Line a 20 x 30cm traybake tin with baking paper and place it in the freezer to chill • Microwaveable bowl and microwave or saucepan and a heatproof bowl • Food processor

Melt the chocolate • Roughly chop the chocolate and place it in the microwaveable bowl • Either melt it in the microwave in 30-second blasts or pour hot water into the bottom of a saucepan and bring to a simmer, put the bowl on top of the pan and leave the chocolate to melt • Once melted, add half the syrup and mix until smooth • Set aside to cool slightly

Blend the mixture • Put the plant-based butter and the rest of the syrup in the food processor and blend for about 2 minutes until creamy • Add the cooled chocolate mixture, then blend for 1 minute until smooth • Scrape the mixture into a large bowl

Create the rocky road • Roughly break up 90g of the pretzels • Roughly snap 230g of the Oreos and 60g of the ginger nuts • Add the rubble to the bowl with the chocolate along with the Rice Krispies • Fold everything together until well coated

Remove the tin from the freezer • Tip the rocky road mixture into the tin and spread it to the edges, pressing down and into the corners to help compact the mixture • Roughly chop the remaining pretzels, Oreos and ginger nuts • Sprinkle over the top of the mixture

Set the rocky road • Freeze for 10–15 minutes • Slice into bars to serve

Red Velvet Sorbet

A proper grown-up tasting dessert, this one will bring out the inner sophistication in even the most outlandish individual. There's just something incredibly classy about deep, dark-coloured desserts. It's essentially a twist on a 'nice cream', but with hints of chocolate, oats and maple sweetness and a beautifully rich red colour courtesy of the beetroot. If you're looking for a speedy pud that's perfect for a romantic date night, this sorbet is just the ticket – brownie points are absolutely guaranteed. One word of warning though... leave your white shirt in the wardrobe – drips will be a nightmare to wash out!

Serves 4

110ml beetroot, dark berry
    or grape juice
2 tbsp jumbo oats
2 tbsp maple syrup
2 tbsp olive oil
50g cocoa powder
400g frozen berries (ideally
    cherries or blueberries;
    mixed berries also work),
    plus a few extra

To serve
30g dark chocolate

Food processor • Microplane or fine grater (optional) • Chill 4 serving glasses in the freezer

Prepare • Put the juice, oats, maple syrup and oil into a food processor • Pulse until smooth • Stir in the cocoa powder and frozen berries • Blend again until smooth and creamy • Taste for sweetness, adding more maple syrup if you like

Serve • Scoop immediately into the chilled glasses • Grate or break up the chocolate • Scatter the chocolate and a few frozen berries on top

Frying Pan Cookie

That's right, we went there... the one-pan cookie. BOOM! Make sure you use the correct-sized pan – you need the cookie to be thin so that you can get it cooked super speedily. (If your pan is smaller than 22cm, it will take a few minutes longer to bake.) A great tip is to remove the cookie from the oven slightly before it looks done, as it will continue to cook in the pan and you don't want to lose that gorgeous, gooey centre. This is a great one to play around with, using your favourite ingredients.

Serves 8

160g light muscovado
    or soft light brown sugar
90g caster sugar
100g plant-based butter, plus
    extra for greasing
110g cold coconut oil
75g tahini
1 tsp ground cinnamon
1 tsp vanilla extract
225g plain flour
1 tsp baking powder
90g large dark-chocolate chunks
90g pecans or blanched hazelnuts
2 tbsp maple syrup (optional)

To serve
dairy-free vanilla ice cream

Preheat oven to 180°C • Grease a 25cm ovenproof frying pan or 25cm round cake tin • Hand-held beaters or stand mixer • Sieve

Make the cookie batter • Crumble any lumps out of the sugars and add them to a bowl along with the butter • Beat until light and fluffy • Add chunks of the solid coconut oil and beat in, along with 15g of the tahini, the cinnamon and vanilla, until just combined • Sieve in the flour and baking powder and beat again until just combined • Fold in half of the chocolate and half of the nuts

Bake the cookie • Tip the batter into the prepared pan and spread it to the edges • Sprinkle the remaining chocolate chips and nuts on top • Bake for 20 minutes • Remove from the oven (it may still be a bit soft, but will continue to firm up as it cools) and leave to cool for 5–10 minutes

Serve • Serve warm or cooled to room temperature • Drizzle over the remaining tahini and the maple syrup before serving sliced or straight from the pan, with scoops of vanilla ice cream

Drinks

06

Blueberry Cheesecake Shake

Is it a dessert? Is it a drink? No, it's a Blueberry Cheesecake Shake and it's come to tickle your taste buds. If you're a die-hard cheesecake fan and you're partial to the occasional milkshake, this is for you. If you make this, be sure to snap a picture and get it on the 'gram, it'd be rude not to!

Serves 4

50g digestive biscuits
30g Demerara sugar (granulated or caster are also fine, if that's what you have)
550ml almond milk
200g dairy-free cream cheese
2 tsp vanilla extract
200g frozen blueberries
60g caster sugar
60g almond butter
ice

Food processor (optional) • **Nutribullet or other power blender** • **4 tall glasses**

Crush the biscuits • Put the biscuits in the food processor and pulse to finely crush them (or put them in a bag and bash them with a rolling pin) • Stir in the Demerara sugar

Blend the cheese mixture • Pour 400ml of the almond milk into the blender • Add the cream cheese and vanilla and blend until smooth • Pour into a separate container

Blend the blueberry mixture • Pour the remaining 150ml of almond milk into the blender • Add the blueberries and caster sugar • Blend until well combined

Assemble • Roughly smear the insides of the glasses with the almond butter • Add a handful of ice to each glass • Reserving some of the crushed biscuit for garnish, divide half of the cheese mixture, then half of the crushed biscuits, then half of the blueberry mixture, between the glasses, in layers • Add some more ice to each glass, then repeat the layers once more • Scatter over the reserved biscuit crumbs

My Body's A Temple Elixir

The old adage 'an apple a day keeps the doctor away' should be updated to: 'a green juice a day keeps the doctor away'. They're delicious, refreshing and healthy. If you're fond of a green juice, or you just want to drink something that's really good for you, this little beauty is for you. The aromatics add a wonderfully fresh and fragrant note to this delicious beverage.

Serves 2

2 small pears
1 lime
140g cucumber
60g spinach leaves
handful of fresh mint leaves
handful of fresh coriander leaves
30ml maple syrup
200ml water

For the aromatics
2 lemongrass stalks
1 kaffir lime leaf (optional)
6 cardamom pods

To garnish
handful of mixed fresh berries
ice

Chill 2 tumblers • Nutribullet or other power blender

Prepare the juice • Cut a few thin slices from the pears and reserve them for later • Roughly chop the rest • Zest half the lime and add it to the smoothie maker, then halve the lime and squeeze in the juice from both halves • Cut a few slices of cucumber and reserve them for garnish, then roughly chop the rest • Reserve a few mint and coriander leaves and roughly chop the rest • Add all the juice ingredients to the smoothie maker and blend until very smooth

Infuse with the aromatics • Roughly chop the lemongrass and lime leaf, if using • Crush the cardamom pods with the flat of a knife • Add the aromatics to the juice and blend very briefly, just to roughly break them all up • Transfer to the fridge to infuse for 15 minutes

Serve • Set a few berries aside for garnishing and roughly chop the rest • Add the reserved pear slices, cucumber and the chopped berries to the chilled glasses along with some ice • Strain the juice, then pour it into the glasses • Garnish with the reserved herbs and the remaining berries

G & Tea Spritz

G&T has become an incredibly popular tipple and swanky bars have a plethora of ways to fancify it – with limited-edition gin, infused tonic, herbs and fresh fruit. We enjoy the occasional posh G&T, so we decided to develop our own. It's dry, sharp, floral, earthy and incredibly refreshing – a real winner on a sunny summer's day!

Makes 2

2 x jasmine tea bags
1 x green tea bag
25g caster sugar
50ml boiling water
5 sprigs of fresh rosemary
    and/or thyme
50ml gin
1 lemon
1 blood orange or pink grapefruit
2 handfuls of ice
200–250ml soda water

Kettle boiled • 2 highball glasses • Sieve or strainer • Stirrer

Prepare the infusion • Put the teabags, sugar and boiling water into a mug or jug • Stir and leave to steep for 5 minutes • Add 3 of the herb sprigs and the gin • Leave to infuse for 12 minutes

Make the spritz • Halve the fruit, cut some slices of each and place them inside the glasses along with some ice • Squeeze over the juice of the remaining fruit • Add the remaining herb sprigs • Strain the tea-infused gin into the glasses and top up with soda • Stir

Peanut Ice Coffee

Coffee, wonderful coffee. In colder months, it's all about warm oat-milk lattes, but in summer, iced coffee takes centre stage. This peanutty twist on a Vietnamese iced coffee is absolutely wonderful. It's a sweet, nutty and creamy treat for a balmy summer afternoon.

Makes 1

40ml hot espresso (strong) coffee
115ml oat milk
2 tbsp maple or golden syrup
30g smooth peanut butter
½ tsp vanilla extract
2 handfuls of ice
30g dairy-free ice cream

To garnish
a few roasted peanuts,
    a coffee bean and
    cocoa powder (optional)

Nutribullet or other power blender • Highball glass

Prep the different elements • Brew the coffee • Add 100ml of the oat milk, the syrup, peanut butter and vanilla extract to the blender • Blend until smooth and foamy • Fill the glass with ice and pour in the blended peanut milk • Add the ice cream to the blender along with the remaining tablespoon of oat milk and blend until smooth

Finish the coffee • Pour the hot coffee into the glass • Top with the ice cream mixture • Chop the peanuts, if using, and sprinkle them over the top with a coffee bean and a dusting of cocoa powder

Rosé Sangria

If you're lucky enough to have an outdoor space and you're hosting a summer shindig you need to make this. It's classy, fruity, refreshing, and if you drink a couple of glasses you'll definitely get the giggles. We're not shy of the occasional alcoholic beverage, but we're always mindful to drink responsibly. We thoroughly recommend you do, too!

Serves 4–6

225g fresh rhubarb
50g caster sugar
200g fresh mixed berries
½ pink lady or red dessert apple
1 lemon
1 x 75cl bottle rosé wine
200ml apple juice

To serve
ice

Medium saucepan over a medium heat • Large jug

Cook the rhubarb • Cut the rhubarb into finger-sized batons • Add to the saucepan along with the sugar and mix well • Cook for about 6 minutes until tender but the rhubarb still holds its shape, stirring occasionally to make sure the rhubarb is coated with sugar syrup • Pour into the jug and transfer to the fridge to cool

Finish the sangria • Once cool, add the berries and roughly break them up with a spoon • Slice the apple and add it to the jug • Thickly peel the lemon zest into the jug • Slice the lemon in half and squeeze in the juice • Pour in the wine and apple juice and mix well

Serve • Pour into glasses filled with ice

Deep South Dirty Martini

Henry holidayed one summer in America's Deep South (on a party boat called *Holy Ship*). He was introduced to the all-American love of all things pickled, including a cocktail called 'What A Pickle'. This is our take on that cocktail, with the bold, grown-up taste of a dirty Martini: sweetened, soured and spiced with a combination of pickled chillies and apple juice. Not for the faint-hearted. Well worth a try.

Serves 2

50ml vermouth
100ml gin or vodka
2 tbsp pickled chilli brine
2 tbsp olive brine
2 tbsp clear apple juice
ice

To garnish
2 pickled chillies
2 olives
2 lemon slices (optional)

Chill 2 Martini glasses • Jug or cocktail shaker

Prepare • Add the vermouth, gin or vodka, brines and apple juice to a jug or cocktail shaker along with some ice • Stir to combine

Serve • Pour into the chilled glasses • Garnish each with a pickled chilli, olive and lemon slice, if using

Margarita Fizz

If you're a fan of the flavours usually associated with Mexican cuisine, this drink is gonna be for you. The lemon and salt provide a satisfying zing, the tequila is warming and earthy, and the agave brings some much needed sweetness. Serve this Margarita with a portion of tasty tacos on a balmy summer's evening and your day will be made.

Serves 4

4 tsp sea salt flakes
4 tsp agave syrup (or preferred syrup)
1 tsp water
4 ice cubes (optional)
4 scoops lemon sorbet
4 x 15ml shots tequila
1 lime
400ml Prosecco or Asti Spumante

Put 4 Martini glasses in the freezer to chill for 15 minutes

Prepare • Spread the salt flakes over a saucer • Put the syrup and water in another saucer and mix • Dip the rim of each chilled glass first in the syrup to coat, then in the salt

Serve • Add an ice cube, if using, and a generous scoop of lemon sorbet to each glass • Add a shot of tequila to each and roughly mix to combine • Cut the lime into slices and add a few to each glass • Top up with Prosecco or Asti Spumante

De La Seoul Bloody Mary

Ah, Sunday mornings – how we love you. With a slightly sore head and a vague sense of guilt, we'll often resort to a veggie roast and a cheeky Bloody Mary to round off the weekend. Try pimping yours up, like we do, with a bit of gochujang or sriracha, Henderson's Relish and stem ginger. Fiery and red. Sweet and bitter. And dressed to kill.

Serves 2

500ml tomato juice
1–4 tsp gochujang or sriracha
1 tsp soy sauce, or to taste
1 tsp Henderson's Relish
   or mushroom ketchup
squeeze of lemon juice
1 ball stem ginger
100ml vodka
ice

To garnish

1 tbsp sesame seeds
2 celery sticks
2 lemon slices
red pepper flakes (optional)
syrup from the stem ginger jar
pickled ginger (optional)

Put 2 highball glasses in the fridge to chill • Small frying pan over a medium-high heat • Nutribullet or other power blender

Start with the garnish • Sprinkle the sesame seeds into the hot frying pan and toast until golden • Spread over a saucer and sprinkle with a few pinches of red pepper flakes, if using • Pour some of the syrup from the stem ginger into another saucer • Dip the rims of the glasses first in the ginger syrup, then into the sesame seeds to coat • Set aside

Make the cocktail • Put the tomato juice, gochujang or sriracha, soy sauce, relish or ketchup, lemon juice and stem ginger into the blender • Blend until smooth • Taste and add more gochujang, sriracha, soy sauce, relish, ketchup or lemon juice to taste • Add the vodka and some ice and shake

Serve • Fill the glasses with ice • Trim the celery and put a stick in each glass • Pour in the cocktail • Add the lemon slices and more red pepper flakes, if you like • Finish with a few pickled ginger slices

Bitter Sweet Peachy Bellini

We do like bubbles! Kombucha (or 'booch', as it's affectionately named) has garnered something of a following in hipster London, where we unashamedly live. It's packed full of live probiotics, it's great for your gut, and has a bittersweet taste. We've paired it with sweet peach, sour lemon and fizzy bubbles to create a wonderful summer party drink. Try to find sweet, ripe peaches for the best flavour.

Serves 2 (with a little extra
    for topping up!)

1 large peach
1 lemon
50ml kombucha
1 tbsp agave syrup or golden syrup
200ml Champagne (or Prosecco
    or Cava)

To garnish
1 peach
1 lemon

Chill 2 champagne glasses • Nutribullet or other power blender

Prepare • Halve the peach, remove the stone and roughly chop • Halve the lemon and squeeze the juice into the blender • Add the chopped peach, kombucha and syrup • Blend until smooth and foamy

Serve • Divide the smoothie mixture between the chilled glasses • Top up with Champagne • Cut the other peach and lemon into slices, garnishing the glasses with a slice of each

PBJ Colada

Peanut butter and jam might be our favourite sweet flavour combination. In fact, Ian has peanut butter and jam on toast for his breakfast about fifty per cent of the time. When we were thinking about the drinks we wanted to include in this book, we got a bit obsessed with the idea of a PBJ-flavoured alcoholic drink. After much deliberation, we decided that the best way to get PBJ into a drink was in the form of a creamy, frothy cocktail. If you like PBJ as much as Ian does, do yourself a favour and rustle up some of these. They're absolutely DELICIOUS!

Serves 2

50g mixed fresh berries (cherries, strawberries or raspberries)
2 heaped tbsp raspberry or strawberry jam
80g peanut butter
200ml unsweetened plant-based milk
1 tsp vanilla extract
1 tbsp caster sugar
50ml dark rum
ice

To garnish
50g mixed fresh berries (cherries, strawberries or raspberries)

Chill 2 tumblers • Nutribullet or other power blender

Prepare the first layer • Put the 50g berries into a small bowl • Add the jam and roughly mash with a fork • Divide the mixture between the glasses and top up with ice until half full

Add the second layer • Put the peanut butter and half the milk into the blender and blend • Pour into the glasses over the berry mixture

Add the third layer • Put the rest of the milk, the vanilla, sugar and rum into the blender and blend until smooth and foamy • Pour into the glasses

Serve • Top with extra berries

Drunken Hot Chocolate

If you like sweet, warm, creamy, chocolatey beverages that have a naughty, but incredibly nice, twist, you're gonna have to make this. It's the perfect drink to cuddle up with while you watch a movie in front of a warm open fire, with big snuggly socks on. Chocolatey: check, warming: check, sweet: check, boozy: check. Just add Netflix.

Serves 3–4

20g hazelnuts
140g dark chocolate
400ml hazelnut milk
1 heaped tsp jumbo oats
5 tsp almond butter
3 tbsp caster sugar
1 tsp vanilla extract
100ml Baileys Almande
50ml whisky or dark rum

Put 2 small mugs in the fridge to chill • Frying pan • Microwaveable bowl and microwave or saucepan and a heatproof bowl • Nutribullet or other power blender • Small saucepan

Toast the hazelnuts • Put the frying pan over a medium–high heat • Add the nuts and toast until golden • Take off the heat and set aside to cool, then chop

Melt the chocolate • Roughly chop the chocolate and place 40g in the microwaveable bowl • Either melt in the microwave in 30-second blasts or pour hot water into the bottom of a saucepan and bring to a simmer, put the bowl on top of the pan and leave the chocolate to melt

Dip the mugs • Put the chopped hazelnuts in a saucer • Dip the mugs into the bowl of chocolate to coat the rims, then into the hazelnuts • Place the mugs back in the fridge to chill again

Make the drinks • Add half the milk to the blender along with the oats and almond butter • Blend until very smooth • Put a small saucepan over a medium–low heat • Pour in the rest of the milk, then add the sugar and vanilla to the pan and heat until hot, but don't let it boil • Add the remaining chocolate • Mix until melted and smooth • Add the blended milk mixture, Baileys and whisky or rum, then mix until smooth and warm

Serve • Take the chilled mugs out of the fridge • Pour the drunken hot chocolate into the mugs

Breakfasts

07

Berry Buckwheat Pancake Stack

These quick and tasty American-style buckwheat pancakes are the perfect weekend breakfast treat. The polenta adds some lovely crunch to the outside and the banana in the batter is a great binder and natural sweetener. We like to add some blueberries for lovely pops of colour and zingy sweetness.

Serves 2

145g buckwheat flour
15g fine polenta (optional)
150g unsweetened plant-based milk
2 tbsp water
2 tbsp rapeseed oil
1 banana
1 tsp vanilla extract
½ tsp baking powder
pinch of salt
handful of fresh blueberries
1 tbsp plant-based butter,
    or more as needed

For the salted orange maple sauce
1 orange
4 tbsp maple syrup
pinch of salt

For the toppings
30g fresh blueberries, raspberries,
    sliced banana or other fruit
handful of nuts or seeds
1 tsp ground cinnamon

Preheat oven to 100°C • Put a serving plate in the oven • Whisk • Large frying pan • Microplane or fine grater • Small saucepan

Make the batter • Weigh the flour, polenta, if using, milk, water and oil into a mixing bowl • Whisk until you have a smooth, thick batter • Peel and add the banana, mashing it into the batter with the prongs of the whisk • Add the vanilla, baking powder, salt and blueberries and stir until well incorporated

Fry the pancakes Put the frying pan over a medium-high heat • Melt the plant-based butter in the pan • Add a ladleful of batter to the pan • Fry for about 3 minutes until brown on the bottom, then flip and fry the other side • Transfer to the warmed plate in the oven while you cook the rest, adding extra butter to the pan when necessary

Meanwhile, make the sauce • Zest and juice the orange • Put the small saucepan over a low heat • Add the maple syrup, orange juice and zest and the salt • Stir and warm through

Serve • Stack the pancakes and pour over the warm sauce • Scatter over your chosen fruit and some nuts or seeds • Dust the cinnamon over the top

Breakfast Hash Tacos

Thanks to our friends at Club Mexicana in London and Piña in Sheffield, we've developed a taste for great-quality tacos. Given that we can't get enough of them, we thought that tacos for breakfast seemed like a good idea and this recipe is the result. Vibrant and packed full of punchy flavour, these are the perfect weekend pick-me-up and a great way to start the day!

Serves 4 (2 tacos each)

200g new potatoes
200g mushrooms
    (preferably chestnut)
4 plant-based sausages
2 tbsp olive oil
8 corn tortillas
1 ripe avocado
200g cherry tomatoes
4 spring onions
1 garlic clove
2 tsp fajita seasoning
100g fresh spinach
a bunch of fresh coriander
salt and black pepper

For the pickled red onions
1 red onion
3 tbsp red wine vinegar
big pinch of salt
big pinch of sugar

To serve
2 limes
hot sauce (optional)

Microwaveable bowl • Clingfilm • Microwave • Large frying pan • Medium frying pan • Clean tea towel • Microplane or fine grater

Pickle the onions • Peel and finely slice the red onion and add to a bowl • Add the vinegar, salt and sugar and toss to combine, squeezing them firmly with your fingers • Set aside

Cook the potatoes • Chop the potatoes into 1–2cm chunks and put them into the microwaveable bowl • Cover with clingfilm and microwave for 5 minutes until soft

Meanwhile, cook the mushrooms and sausages • Slice the mushrooms and roughly chop the sausages • Put the large frying pan over a high heat and add the oil • Add the sausages to the hot oil and stir roughly to break them up • Add the mushrooms and pinch of salt • Fry for 5 minutes, stirring occasionally

Make the tacos • Put the medium frying pan over a high heat • When the pan is hot, drop in a tortilla and toast for about 15 seconds • Flip and toast for another 15 seconds • Transfer to a plate and cover with a tea towel • Repeat with the remaining tortillas

Prep the veg • Halve and stone the avocado, peel and slice the flesh, place in a bowl and set aside • Cut the limes into wedges • Quarter the cherry tomatoes • Slice the spring onions

Finish the hash • Take the potatoes out of the microwave and toss them into the sausage pan • Peel the garlic then grate it directly into the pan • Sprinkle over the fajita seasoning • Cook for 2 minutes • Add the fresh spinach and cook until wilted • Add the chopped cherry tomatoes and half the spring onions • Season to taste • Remove from the heat

Serve • Shape the tortillas into pockets in your hands and fill them with hash • Top with picked onions, sliced avocado, hot sauce, if using, fresh coriander and the remaining spring onions • Serve with the lime wedges for squeezing over alongside

Em-J's Miracle Morning Porridge

Henry and his fiancée Em-J like to practise 'miracle mornings', ticking off a load of mindful goodness, like exercise, meditation and gratitude, before the day begins. Yes, it's a cliché, but it makes them feel great! Eating this porridge is the final task of the morning. Here are some of their favourite combinations. Try them all and then freestyle your own! Ommmmm.

Makes enough for
1 big or 2 small bowls

60g porridge oats
285ml oat milk

Small saucepan • Frying pan on a medium heat

Make the porridge • In a small saucepan, cover the oats with the milk and bring to the boil over a medium heat, stirring constantly • Reduce the heat and continue to stir for 1– 2 minutes until you have creamy porridge

Chocolate Orange Porridge

1 tbsp cocoa powder
1 tbsp maple syrup
1 orange or blood orange
1 tsp dried chilli flakes (optional)
cacao nibs or dairy-free
    chocolate sprinkles
pinch of sea salt

When the porridge is cooked, stir through the cocoa powder and maple syrup • Zest the orange, set the zest aside, then cut the orange in half • Squeeze the juice from one half into the porridge and cut the other half into slices, removing the rind from around the edges • Tip the chocolate porridge into a bowl and top with the orange slices, zest, cacao nibs or chocolate sprinkles, sea salt and the chilli flakes, if you fancy some heat!

Peanut Butter Power Porridge

1 tbsp peanut butter
1 banana
2 tbsp pecans, hazelnuts
    or almonds, or a mix
handful of goji berries

When the porridge is cooked, stir through the peanut butter • Slice the banana • Top the porridge with the banana slices, nuts and goji berries

Super-Seeded Porridge

handful of your favourite
    mixed seeds (sesame,
    linseeds, sunflower,
    pumpkin, nigella)
pinch of sea salt
1 tsp maple syrup
1 tsp vanilla paste
generous handful of fresh berries

Put the seeds in the hot dry frying pan with the salt • Toast until they pop • When the porridge is cooked, stir through the maple syrup and vanilla paste • Top with the berries and sprinkle over the toasted seeds

PEANUT BUTTER
POWER PORRIDGE

CHOCOLATE
ORANGE
PORRIDGE

SUPER-SEEDED
PORRIDGE

Greens & Caper Crumb

Getting sick of avocado on toast? There are so many other amazing greens you can pile up on toast for breakfast, lunch and supper. Feel free to play around with your favourites here: kale, spring greens, spinach, Tenderstem broccoli – go for it! While leaves and peas can go straight in the pan, green beans and broccoli will need a quick 3-minute steam or blanch. Frying dark leafy greens turns them a wonderful bright green colour and maintains their crunch, then the parmesan melts into the leaves and caramelises slightly in the pan. The caper crumble is a great speedy way to add zing and texture.

Serves 2

50g green beans or Tenderstem broccoli, asparagus, sugar snaps, or a mixture
1 tbsp plant-based butter
1 tbsp olive oil
100g mixed leafy greens of your choice (cavolo nero, kale, cabbage, spring greens, collard greens, sprout tops, spinach)
50g frozen peas
½ tsp lazy garlic or ½ garlic clove, crushed
25g plant-based parmesan

For the caper crumble
1½ tsp capers (scooped straight from the jar, no need to rinse)
1½ tsp nuts of your choice (e.g. hazelnuts, pecans, almonds, walnuts)
½ fresh green chilli
handful of fresh basil leaves
25g plant-based parmesan
½ lemon

To serve
handful of mixed seeds
2 slices sourdough bread
1 spring onion
plant-based butter

Preheat grill to high or have the toaster ready • Large saucepan of water with a lid, on a high heat with a colander or steamer pan on top • Large frying pan over a medium heat • Microplane or fine grater • Small food processor • Small frying pan

Make the parmesan greens • Add the green beans (or broccoli, etc.) to the colander or steamer pan set over the boiling water, cover and steam for 3 minutes • Add the plant-based butter and olive oil to the hot frying pan • If using greens with tough stalks, such as kale or cavolo nero, pull away the leaves and discard the stalks • Once the pan is sizzling, add the leafy greens and stir to coat well • Add the green beans from the steamer, the peas and the garlic • Grate the parmesan into the pan • Cook, stirring, for about 5 minutes, until everything is dark green and the parmesan is melted and starting to caramelise • Turn off the heat and leave to sit while you make the crumble

Make the caper crumble • Add the capers, nuts, chilli, basil and parmesan to the food processor • Grate in the zest of the lemon half • Pulse a few times until you have a coarse, nutty crumble (just a couple of pulses is fine - be careful not to overdo it).

Toast the seeds • Put a frying pan over a medium-high heat • Scatter over the seeds and toast until golden • Take off the heat

To serve • Toast the bread under the grill or in the toaster • Finely slice the spring onion • Spread the toast with plant-based butter and pile on the parmesan greens • Top with the caper crumble, a squeeze of lemon juice from the zested lemon half, the sliced spring onions and the toasted seeds

Frances' PBJ Pop Tarts

Remember Saturday morning cartoons? And pop tarts? These will take you right back! Ian and his sister Frances used to love the occasional Saturday-morning pop tart when they were kids, so we came up with our own. We made them speedy by using ready-made shortcrust pastry (obvious, right?) and turned again to our favourite sweet American flavour combo: peanut butter and jelly. Epic.

Makes 4

1 x 320g sheet ready-rolled
    dairy-free shortcrust pastry
4 tbsp raspberry jam
1½ tsp plant-based butter
1 tbsp caster sugar

For the peanut butter frosting
4 tbsp icing sugar
3 tbsp smooth peanut butter
2 tbsp unsweetened plant-based milk,
    or more as needed
1 tsp vanilla extract

For the toppings
30g frozen raspberries
30g salted roasted peanuts

Preheat oven to 200°C • Line a baking sheet with baking paper • Sieve • Whisk • Set a cooling rack over a baking tray

Make the tarts • Unroll your pastry sheet with the long edge nearest you and cut vertically into 4 even rectangles • Place 1 tablespoon of jam in the middle of the lower half of each rectangle • Fold the top halves over to form 4 rectangular parcels • Crimp the edges together with a fork to seal in the jam • Make a few holes in the tops of the tarts with a fork to let air escape • Rub the plant-based butter over each parcel and sprinkle with caster sugar • Place on the lined baking sheet and bake in the hot oven for 20 minutes

Meanwhile, make the glaze • Sieve the icing sugar into a bowl and add the peanut butter, plant-based milk and vanilla • Whisk together until smooth, adding a dash more milk if the glaze looks too thick

Prepare the toppings • Crumble the frozen berries into a bowl • Bash the peanuts to crumbs in a pestle and mortar or using a rolling pin

To serve • Remove the tarts from the oven and carefully slide them onto the cooling rack set over a tray • Spoon over the glaze, letting it cover the surface of the tarts and drip down the sides • Sprinkle over the toppings • Tuck in while they're still warm, but be careful as they will be piping hot inside

Kinda Salmon & Cream Cheese Bagels

Coated in spices, grilled and then quickly brined in a delicious combo of capers, nori and citrus, the texture of the carrots in this dish are transformed and the salty, smoky flavours come together in a brilliant approximation of smoked salmon. Pile them high on bagels slathered with cream cheese and you've got yourself one hell of a breakfast!

Makes 2

2 sesame bagels

For the 'salmon'
1 tbsp sesame oil
1 tsp garlic powder
1 tsp smoked paprika
1 tbsp tamari or soy sauce
2 large carrots

For the dressing
½ nori sheet
1 tsp capers
1 tsp caper brine
a squeeze of lemon juice
a squeeze of orange juice

To serve
1 tbsp olive oil
pinch of salt
3 tbsp dairy-free cream cheese
1 spring onion
a few fresh dill fronds
½ lemon

Preheat grill to max • Line a baking tray with baking paper • Frying pan

Start with the 'salmon' • In a large bowl, mix together the oil, garlic powder, smoked paprika and tamari or soy sauce • Peel 2 carrots into ribbons and add them to the bowl, tossing them in the flavoured oil • Arrange the pieces over the lined baking tray and grill for 5 minutes, until starting to brown at the edges

Meanwhile, make the dressing • Crumble the nori sheet into a bowl • Add all the other dressing ingredients and mix together

Finish the 'salmon' • Add the grilled carrots to the bowl of dressing and toss to coat • Transfer to the freezer to chill

Build the bagels • Put the frying pan over a medium heat • Add the olive oil and pinch of salt • Split the bagels and place them, cut-sides down, in the pan • Toast until brown • Spread the bottom half of each bagel with the dairy-free cream cheese • Remove the 'salmon' ribbons from the freezer and arrange them on top of the cream cheese • Finely slice the spring onion • Sprinkle the onions and dill over the carrots • Squeeze over the juice of the lemon and close the bagels with the tops

Giant Breakfast Muffin

For a naughty breakfast, there's 'nuffin' better than a muffin. Thing is, they can be laborious to make. So, in true speedy style, we've hacked it to bring you a muffin that is quick and easy to get on the plate. Rather than faff around with muffin cases, we use a baking tray to make a giant muffin cake, cut it into slices and then adorn it with delicious berries, nuts, syrup and chocolate chips. A truly incredible and indulgent breakfast. Just make sure you have a cup of tea to go with it!

Serves 6

450ml + 1½ tbsp unsweetened
    plant-based milk
20ml cider vinegar
45g oats
60g + 1 heaped tbsp caster sugar
1 tbsp instant coffee powder
260g plain flour
2 level tsp bicarbonate of soda
2 pinches of salt
100g blueberries
50g dark chocolate chips
50g chopped walnuts

To serve
200g mixed berries, roughly sliced
25g dark chocolate chips
    and/or walnuts
plant-based cream or
    plant-based yoghurt
maple or date syrup, for drizzling

Preheat oven to 180°C • Line a 27 x 22cm baking tray or traybake tin with baking paper, letting it hang over the sides • Nutribullet or other power blender

Make the wet mixture • Pour 150ml of the milk into the blender • Add the vinegar and oats and blend for 1–2 minutes until smooth

Make the coffee mixture • In a mug, mix the 1½ tablespoons of milk with 1 heaped tablespoon of sugar and the instant coffee

Make the batter • Mix the flour, bicarbonate of sugar, salt and the 60g sugar in a bowl • Make a well in the middle of the mixture, then pour in the wet mixture along with the remaining 300ml milk • Fold together, but don't over-mix • Pour in the coffee mixture • Add the blueberries, chocolate chips and walnuts and give it 2 more folds

Bake • Scrape the batter into the prepared tin • Bake on the middle shelf of the oven for 12–15 minutes, until golden and puffed up

Serve • Use the lining paper to lift the pancake out of the tin • Drizzle the cream or yoghurt and the syrup over the top, then top with the berries and chocolate chips or walnuts • Cut into slices

Fran's Fruit & Fibre Flapjacks

Who would have thought we could create an even faster flapjack recipe? But we did! We hacked the speed here by roasting the dry mix while creating a wonderful, sticky syrup to bind all the goodness together. These flapjacks are not only quick, they're delicious, filling and incredibly moreish. A go-to recipe in the BOSH! arsenal. As perfected and loved by our good friend Fran, foodie extraordinaire, these flapjacks are delicious, kinda healthy and super speedy.

Makes 12–16

125g jumbo oats
75g desiccated coconut
75g mixed seeds (we used sunflower and linseed but pumpkin would be perfect)
pinch of salt
200g golden syrup
25ml sunflower oil
100g coconut oil
100g peanut butter
100g bran flakes (we used spelt bran flakes)
100g raisins

For the flax egg
4 tbsp ground flaxseeds
8 tbsp warm water

Preheat oven to 180°C • Roasting tin • Food processor • Grease and line a 20 x 20cm baking tin with baking paper

Make the base • Put the oats, coconut, seeds, salt, 25g of the syrup and the sunflower oil in the roasting tin and mix together • Roast in the hot oven for 8 minutes, mixing once or twice, until lightly toasted, keeping an eye on it as the coconut will brown fast

Make the flax egg • Combine the ground flaxseeds and water in a small bowl and mix well • Set aside to rest for 5 minutes

Meanwhile, make the flapjack mixture • Add the rest of the golden syrup, the coconut oil and peanut butter to the food processor and pulse until well combined • Add the bran flakes and toasted base ingredients from the oven and pulse again briefly, until the mixture has started to break down but is not completely smooth • Remove the blade from the processor and add the raisins and flax egg to the mixture • Stir until everything is well combined

Assemble • Scrape the mixture into the lined tin and press out evenly with the spatula • Transfer to the fridge to cool and firm up for at least 30 minutes • Cut into 12–16 squares

Speedy thanks

A quick moment for some big love

Our creative team, who navigated insane deadlines due to lockdown and who put everything they have into making this book look awesome • Lizzie Mayson with Matthew Hague and Stephanie Mcleod for your truly amazing food photography • Nicky Johnston with Matthew Tortolano for photographing us both, and making sure we didn't let the food down • Elena Silcock for your incredible food styling and recipe wizardry, along with Grace Paul, Alice Ostan, Dominique Eloise Alexander and Libby Silbermann • Sarah Birks and Lauren Miller for your excellent prop styling • Lucy Sykes-Thompson for your gorgeous book design • Emily Preece-Morrison and Caroline McArthur for helping make sure we got all the words right • Emily-Jane Williams for your brilliant make-up skill, and Alexis Knox for styling us – you're both masters of your art • Louis & Lucy from Larry King for the A-grade haircuts! • Dan Hurst, the most patient, unflappable, project editor you'll ever meet • And a special thank you to Jude Sharkey, the studio manager at Factory for storing all our stuff for us when Boris announced we'd have to shut the shoot down halfway through

Our amazing food team, who make sure our recipes look amazing and test them to within an inch of their lives, so they turn out perfect for you every time • Rosie French, Katy McClelland, Isla Murray, India Whiley-Morton and Jenna Leiter, you are super creative and talented human beings • Special thanks to Fran Paling and Luke Robinson who helped us do a final cook through of every single dish in ten days • We simply couldn't have got this book over the line without you

Our publishing team at HQ / HarperCollins for making this book happen • Lisa Milton for being an awesome publisher, taking risks and keeping calm as deadlines flew out the window • Rachel Kenny for being the beating heart of the project • Charlie Redmayne for championing us since the very beginning • Kate Oakley for your design skills • Georgina Green, Fliss Porter, Darren Shoffren, Marta Juncosa, Jay Cochrane, Debbie McNally, Kelly Spells and the whole sales team for hustling as hard as ever • Joanna Rose, Janet Asprey, Noleen Robinson, Jen Callahan-Packer, Sophie Calder and Ben Hurd for their brand, marketing and publicity expertise • Abigail Le Marquand-Brown for being a brilliantly enthusiastic assistant • Halema Begum, Charles Light and Sarah Davis for keeping our production and rights firmly under control

Our beloved BOSH! Team, who are on the daily mission with us to get more plants on plates • Cathy, Charlie & Nat, thank you being in it with us every day. There is no BOSH! without you • Em-J for making our faces look pretty and for agreeing to marry Henry • Bev and Sarah for your brilliant management and enabling us to tell our mums we were going to be on the telly • Carver PR, Megan, Sarah & Becca, for banging the PR drum. Only you could get two vegan boys into the Daily Star • Gail for making our brand look awesome and Curly for keeping our copy in check • Bodyweight D for being an awesome housemate and keeping us sane during lockdown • Charles, Andrea and Christine for your financial savvy • Guy Mottershead for your brilliant team work, and putting us on supermarket shelves

Henry's fam • Jane & Mark • Alice & Graham • Chris, Paul & Tom Williams • Sukey, Nick, Gus & Arthur • Claire, Nick & Xander • Alison & Curtis • John Dodd, Zoe & Stanley • Davey P

Ian's fam • Mum, Dad, Frances, Stew & Bump • Carolyn, Edward & Philip • Robin & Suzie • Simon • Josephine, Katie, Mike & Kev • Steve, Shirley, Lynsey & Kerry

Our amazing friends • Alex & Tara • Nat, Khairan & Lennox • Marcus, Ellie, Jasper, Caspian & Nia • Ekow, Claire, Hugo & Xander • Zulf, Farhana, Ayza & Ayla • Alex Farbz, Cat, Freddie & Samuel • Addison, Claire, Lola Grace & Stanley • Kweku, Angie & Bump • Tom, Emilie, Alex & Ruby • Martha, Duncan & Ernie • Josh, Charlotte, Leo & Uma • Tim, Susie, Wren & Ember • Anna & Beth • Nick & Ruth • Maso, Bex & Finn • Tom, Stef & Romy • Chris • Luke & Kasia • Nish • Janey • Joe • Ted • Jenny • Louis • Mutty • Leslie • Ayo • AK • Fallon, Tess & Dee • Natalia • Danielle • Sophie • Kate • Robbie & Klaus • Damian & Judy • Derek • JP & Alex • Rupy • Adam & Joe

And thank *you* for picking up this book. We remain so grateful that you would invite us to be part of your life and your kitchen. It's an absolute privilege to share food with you • A special thank you to our super loyal fans in the Team BOSH! group, who go out of their way to cook our food and share it with others. Seeing your creations daily means the world to us • And to everyone who follows us on our social media channels – you made us and we are completely, utterly and eternally grateful for you, your time and your attention. We hope you all enjoy this book as much as we enjoyed creating it for you

Index

Watch cookalong recipe videos and
start your plant-based meal plan at
www.bosh.tv

BOSH!
TV